THE LIFE AND BANISHMENT OF APOPHIS

THE LIFE AND BANISHMENT OF APOPHIS

Matthew Petchinsky

The Life and Banishment of Apophis
By: Matthew Edward Petchinsky

Memories translated and channeled by: Apophis

BOOK 1

Message from Apophis

Many Of you may know me as the "devil of ancient Egypt". However, this is not true, all you know about me is a lie. The lie has been spread to cause fear of me by those in the Council that I have mentioned throughout this book. I just want you all to know I am truly peaceful. I don't eat the sun or souls as those lies that you have been fed for thousands of years. I have been for the last three hundred years in your history, these stories you are about to read is how I went through different events. You may have heard of others that are channeled by others, there is a chance they are creation of the Council to mislead you. I know I am me. My story must be told. I want you to understand that I am not a destructive force, I never was since the beginning. The story you are about to read is what I can remember, I don't exactly remember the names of the hosts because there are so many over 3 centuries.

Who is the Council?

The Council is made up of all pantheons of gods and goddesses, across all ancient societies from Mesopotamia, Greek, Roman, Celtic, Egyptian, Hindu, Chinese, and so forth.

The Egyptian gods created it to control this world, however, they were in control before they were classified as their current names. They are much older than you believe. They created and destroyed many lifeforms. All lifeforms serve one purpose to them as playthings like a child does with toys. The Council believes themselves to be the only higher beings, but their arrogance is astonishing to say the least. They have banished thousands of others, like me. They place rules on all banished, things get worse for you if you don't follow the rules. You may ask "if they are so powerful, why don't they try to stop you from writing this?" Answer: they have tried even now since I had some assistance in wiping them out for the moment. They are still trying. The creatures they created to whisper in the ears of mankind. Ever hear a voice telling you to do something bad? Like killer type bad? Well, that is the Council's creature, that whispered that in your mind.

I had a run in with quite a few of these things and destroyed some of them, but they have a few subspecies type of these creatures. I know the Council will return in 1,000 years' time, but there has been leaks thanks to those creatures the Council has created. The council wants you to be mindless of this, I am here to inform and help you.

-Apophis

Prologue

Most origin stories of Demons, Devils, Gods and Goddesses all begin to where they are all created from one superior being, and most of them have untold stories and lives beyond small legends.

Many are completely forgotten throughout time; others just slumber until awoken by a great desire of hatred or protection. Which not all are made to protect but to destroy. Many are forced to live a life of banishment within a human host. Now, this from the eyes of an outsider looks mental and madness and must be cured by pills or exorcisms, but you can't cure or remove them in such ways. They are placed in the body to help the host and live out a punishment. Even when others forbid them from helping the host.

As in this case of Apophis, he has lived a great life until he was betrayed.

So, let's begin the story no one for the last 30,000 years has ever known......

Chapter One: the birth of Apophis

Apophis was a creation of himself, he willed himself into existence. Most other stories would say he was born of the fire of some dust or something, but this isn't true. He was like RA a self-made being as well. Now, Apophis wasn't some truly all peaceful being or a completely Evil, vile one like he is commonly portrayed in the Egyptian mythology.

Yes, he was against Ra, like the inscriptions depict, he was against Ra for a different reason, as he is of the other members of the Egyptian pantheon. Apophis and RA are true enemies because they have a difference of right and wrong. RA ran the Council of Gods of every pantheon that is responsible for every issue in this world. Apophis didn't believe the evil the council created was right. They don't like anyone opposing them.

Before the banishment, Apophis was in his domain in the section of lower Egypt, he like to shapeshift at times, He usually was that of a great serpent, but he takes many forms. One of Apophis's favorites is that of a 20-year-old with black hair the flow like the Nile River, muscles that were at an impressive size not too exaggerated, a serpent's necklace with red ruby jewels for eyes, his serpent eyes were hard to mask, but he used a spell to make everyone believe he had beautiful amber brown eyes.

While he was in his human form, he gathered quite a large following of people and he had been flirting and mating with the most beautiful mortal women of his followers. Now, those children that were conceived in secret, Men and Gods didn't know of this because it was forbidden on both sides.

Each of the children became Apophis's minion and soldiers for his army. These children were extremely unique and special that they fully matured to their adult size within a month due to Apophis's serpent gene and God gene within each of them.

Apophis was at 12,000 soldiers when he planned to go against the council to have their power and create a better world, the evil and darkness in this world was because of The Council. Apophis wanted to change that under his rule for the rest of time and creation hung in the balance. He wanted the rule of the serpent to last forever.

Apophis was not only going to attack the Egyptian pantheon, but all other pantheons from throughout the world, once his army had grown in strength.

RA caught wind of this plan and employed Seth the original God of Chaos to go the mortal realm and to take the form of Apophis to cause chaos.

Seth agreed to take the form of Apophis and he went town to a small town on the out skirts of lower Egypt, Seth in the form of Apophis began to cause death and destruction in the form of Apophis. Seth turned everything into sand with his touch and he cause the small village to disappear as sand with every living creature and human being turning to sand. The power to turn everything into sand by touch wasn't a power of Apophis. If Apophis were to destroy a village, Apophis would have eaten and burned everything without a tract.

RA witnessed the events that transpired in the village of the lost, he became enraged, he then called a meeting amongst the rest of The Council, and they came to the plan to capture Apophis and put him on trial. Apophis didn't know what was about to happen to him.

Chapter 2: The Trial of Apophis

Apophis was slumbering on his star bed, when he was rudely awoken by the goddess MA'AT, the winged sky goddess of truth and justice. She approached Apophis with her guards and soldiers. They snatched Apophis from his star bed and dragged away without a word. Apophis was to be taken in front of The Council for trial. His captors didn't say a word to him as they entered to Council chamber.

Apophis was confused on why he was being dragged in front of the council. Apophis looked around and saw hundreds possibly thousands of eyes staring down on him, all the pantheons of Gods and Goddesses were there, waiting to hear the trial of Apophis.

Everyone was silent in the Council chamber, so quiet that you could hear the dust fall to the floor. RA stepped out from his chamber; he stepped forward on his balcony that was just above Apophis three stories high from where Apophis was at. Apophis looked up towards RA. RA is the head leader of the Council, his beak glistened as he was walking towards the edge of the balcony and as he looked down upon Apophis.

"Apophis, you are hereby charged with the guilt of destroying 100,000 innocent lives of a small village in lower Egypt by turning them to sand." RA roared down from his high place.

Before Apophis could speak the truth and say it was not him nor does he possess such power to turn any thing living thing nor nonliving thing into sand. Ra continued.

"The Council has decided for you to be imprisoned and banished in different human bodies and different lives for one thousand years." RA roared down from his high place not hesitating at all to give sentence to Apophis.

Apophis turned around as a large platform door opened in the middle of the Council chamber floor. As large crystal was rising from the opening in the floor, the crystal was the shape of a pyramid and the size of a small pyramid, possibly a little smaller than that. The crystal was a solid quartz crystal with an amethyst cut at the top of the crystal pyramid.

Apophis stared at the crystal pyramid; he knew something bad was about to happen to him. Within a few seconds, the pyramid was warming up, chains came from the floor to subdue Apophis and keep him from running away, these chains were a strong diamond and obsidian mixture, unbreakable in nature.

The crystal pyramid shined bright like a thousand suns, until it released a beam of light that encompassed Apophis, the light burned and started to rip Apophis's flesh and bones apart. Apophis screamed in agony; the Council just watch as the process was being done. RA grinned at the enjoyment of Apophis's torment.

While Apophis was being sentenced to his banishment, his children were being slaughtered, 10,000 of them were killed by the Council's soldiers. The last 2,000 ran for safety and they would travel the world in the search of Apophis for what they believed was their abandonment. They built a rage and hatred of Apophis the likes of which the council couldn't have planned better.

Chapter 3: The Awakening of Apophis.

Unknown host #1

Apophis had awoken within a host somewhere in England. Apophis was still dazed from the crystal pyramid's immense power, he still felt the burning sensation from his flesh, but he wasn't of flesh no more. He was of essence like a ghost possessing a body. Apophis didn't understand why this had happened to him.

Apophis remembers being in a young child's body, the year was about 1784. Apophis could see everything that his host child could see. Apophis didn't want to frighten the child, so he limited his control and stayed in the back of the mind of the child. He would wait until the child was a bit older to take full control for a long period of time. Apophis saw that the family he was in was on family-owned farm just outside of London. **(Since I don't recall the name of the host, because there are so many, I will use other names for the hosts that I am about to share with you. My banishment has been long and painful. I must warn you that the memories are traumatic. Now for the names, because there are dialogue pieces, we will use pseudonyms for each host-Apophis).**

Apophis saw Bastet was watching him and the family in the corner of the room, she was standing there with a blank look just staring, observing like any cat does generally. Bastet was unknow to anyone else in the room.

Bastet started walking towards Apophis, her tail was twitching and swaying back and forth as she walked towards Apophis. When everyone left the room, Apophis took control of the child's body and spoke with Bastet.

Bastet told Apophis that he wasn't to help anyone in his host's life or any host for that matter or else be brought in front of the council and more severe measures would be taken such as an elimination of his essence all together by use of the crystal pyramid that sent him through time into the host body.

Other rules include:

-Not telling anyone that you exist

-Not interfering with major events

-No stopping anything the council puts as planned such as a death of a person or fall of a nation.

-No sexual relations with humans for the Council fears of the genetic material from your essence will be transferred over.

Apophis: Yes, these rules are just a few that the council had placed on me and others that are banished like me. If we break more than one rule, we could be wiped out from existence. The Council has used your society and many others like playthings for their entertainment.

Apophis was only there to suffer and learn what it is like to be in a weakly constructed form of being instead of his God form. He was never to interfere with anything his host gets into. Not even if his host was to get angry and start stabbing and killing.

For the purposes of the story, we will call this young host Rupert, as we mentioned we will be using pseudonyms for the hosts.

Bastet looked concerned and she added that she suggested that Apophis help control this hosts anger, even though it would go against the rules, but Bastet was one for protecting children, she didn't want a child to get hurt. It is bothersome to her. Bastet is a protector of cats and children. Apophis was confused on how much anger could a child have? Apophis would soon find out how bad this child's anger and rage would be.

Bastet turned and disappeared leaving Apophis alone in the farm family's home.

Apophis went into hiding in the back of the young host's mind. Apophis witnessed his young host Rupert get into fights with his mother and father and his parents beat him with metal spoons, and piece of wood. Apophis felt all the pains of his host, he didn't realize that there was a connection with his host to where he felt physical pain. Rupert bottled all his rage from the beatings all his life that grew into an uncontrollable rage.

Apophis could not control the rage inside Rupert. This abuse went on for ten long years until the child was eighteen years old.

Ten years later around the time of Rupert's eighteenth birthday, Apophis had witnessed that Rupert had applied and selected to join the army. Rupert had been stationed in India, France, and surprisingly Egypt, knowing how the Council set traps for Apophis for places like Egypt, but this time, the traps were not sprung or was he being watched closely, allowing him to roam in Egypt, probably.

I knew the Council would have been watching me and set traps for me in certain parts of the world, usually these traps include my host to be sick and not being able to do much or sinking a ship. Sometimes there are creatures place in places where I am forbidden to cross. These creatures would attack me and cause harm to me and my host, but my host usually wouldn't understand what was going on. -Apophis.

During the time in Egypt, Rupert became ill and was bed ridden for the better part of a week. Apophis tried his best to take control the best he could for the short moments because of how weak the host body was.

Apophis went and explored on how much Egypt had changed, he had learned that it was controlled by a religious group called the Muslims. Their empire at the time was the Ottoman Empire. He saw religious buildings called Mosques in places where their used to be nothing but sand and land that was empty back in his day. He was in Cairo, Egypt. Apophis was amazed and disappointed at the same time.

Apophis did travel out in the middle of the desert about 10 miles or so to a location that he knew each night. The location he went to was a tomb of his that he had hidden before his banishment. None of the Council knew of his secret tomb.

The tomb was sealed needing a combination lock to unlock, thankfully thousands of years before, Apophis had buried a stone box with an amulet inside.

He dug up the box and open the stone box with an amulet of a serpent that had red eyes from the rubies and yellow topaz stone for the fire breath that the snake was breathing. The amulet was named the "fire of breath".

Apophis used this amulet to open his tomb door. The magic inside the amulet opened the door, all Apophis had to do was to point the amulet to the door. When the door opened stepped forward was a large stone serpent golem. The large serpent golem was growling at him.

Apophis said a command in ancient Egyptian and the beast bowed before him. Apophis walked pasted the guard and entered his tomb, inside the tomb was all the treasures of Apophis, from the gold statues of himself to his jewelry and precious stones.

Apophis felt his home was here in that tomb, he wanted to die in that tomb and be buried along with his tomb and be lost forever, but he knew if he was to try and bury himself there, only his host's body would remain, his soul would go to another host body.

Yes, my grand treasure is still buried out there, I can't be for sure now where is it is, because of the changing sands and the fact that it has been a long time since I've been there. I felt a depression knowing I would never see my treasure again. -Apophis

Apophis looked at the amulet that was now around his neck, he knew that he couldn't take it back with him. Also, the amulet amplified any powers he had back in his time, but now it was useless because the Council had stripped him of all powers. If he took anything back with him to civilization, he would lose his treasure because he would move on to another host body once the host died. He also knew that if anyone got ahold of his treasure, they would end civilization because of the curse he placed upon his treasure to protect it. He Made it where any mortal who touch it would go crazy and lose their mind as well as any mortal who touch it would become extremely ill as well, the disease was uncurable.

Apophis knew the Council did the same thing to ensure their treasures would be protected as well. It was common practice for all gods to give traps like that.

Apophis spent 30 minutes in his tomb until he was ready to head back to the city. When he left, he buried the amulet in the ground in the stone box.

For the next three or four nights while Rupert was stationed in Egypt, Apophis went out to the tomb to feel closer to his own time. He sometimes was deep in thought about how he once had such a grand army of 12,000 soldiers who were also his offspring, but now they were exterminated, he wandered if any of them survived.

One night, when Apophis was on his night excursion back to the tomb, the winds of Egypt started to crackle, and the sand encircled him. Apophis remembered that this was a power of his children. The voices of 2,000 were speaking all at the same time, but Apophis could only understand some of the words.

"Father" "Abandoned" "Betrayed" "Us"

Are the words Apophis could hear. From behind him came a strong blow to the back that knocked him down.

Apophis was shaken that his children were attacking him.

"I didn't abandon or betray you, I was kidnapped and banished." Apophis shouted.

The dust settled and all 2,000 of his children appeared to him. The one standing right in front of Apophis, he stared Apophis right in the eye, The rage Apophis saw was unbearable, that it burned like looking at a flame too long.

"You lie, father. We will hunt you in each life that you will go to. Every Halloween, much like tonight we are stronger than you. You didn't know this?" the head child that was standing in front of Apophis said.

Apophis was shocked that his children had that ability, they must have evolved on their own to use the thinness of the veil between world to gain strength. They have become quite a threat that Apophis had intended so many thousands of years ago. Instead of serving him in battle, they were taking their revenge upon Apophis.

His children each took turns inflicting pain on Apophis for the next hour. When they had finished, they left him there laying in the pitch darkness. Laying there in the sand, Apophis felt pain and disappointment when he learned from now on, he would have to be cautious every Halloween.

As he lay there in the sands in the pitch blackness, he realized he had lost complete control of his children, he wandered if he could ever control them again, since he had seen how much stronger they are now.

Apophis also learned that human pain is very uncomfortable. He realized how fragile human bodies are. He missed his original form, in that form he could heal within a few minutes, but as he is in human form it would take much longer.

After gaining so strength back after laying in the sand and pitch blackness, Apophis began his journey back to Cairo, Egypt. When he arrived back to the room Rupert was assigned at Apophis laid on the bed and went to sleep.

I learned that night so many years ago, that my children retained a rage the likes of which I had not experienced myself. They could have killed my host and I that night, but they knew they would have killed an innocent and I would have been sent to another host before my essence was killed. Yes, you can kill a soul if you have the right powers to do so. -Apophis.

A few years later, Rupert was sent into battle in what would be known as "the war of 1812". The war was with the Americans again, England was still determined to control America.

Apophis watched as many of Rupert's servicemen were killed in battle, Apophis tried to help Rupert fight, but Rupert was killed in battle. Apophis felt the body go cold as everything went black.

Apophis woke up in a blackness, an endless blackness, the blackness was not cold or warm, there was no temperature there. All you do is float in the air there, there is no sun, no sky, no wind, no solid ground which to stand. Apophis had never been in such a place before. He just stayed there alone floating, no way of telling time. One could go completely insane here.

The blackness, I will refer to several times during this book, I have been there, countless time during my last 300 years. Each time a host body dies I end up in the endless blackness. What is the blackness exactly you may be wandering. Well, the endless blackness, a in between world, a sort of void if you wish to call it that. Many of those that end up there, have given up and that is when the council would take them to the large crystal pyramid and wipe them from existence. -Apophis

Unknown host #2

Apophis was floating there in the Eternal Blackness, when a flash of light engulfed him, moments later Apophis woke up in a host body. He stood up and went to the standing mirror that was in the corner of the room. Apophis saw that he was in a female body. The body was skinny with medium sized breasts, brunette hair, and green eyes.

Apophis was amazed at how beautiful his host's body was, Apophis walked away from the mirror and saw a news paper on a table with a mirror on it, and as well assorted makeups. The date on the paper was 1815, three years since his last host. Apophis was amazed on how fast time progressed. In the eternal blackness, you cannot tell time, for Apophis, he felt he was in the Eternal Blackness for five minutes, not three years.

Apophis figured that time on this side of the Eternal Blackness moved faster or is time compressed in the Eternal Blackness. He quickly put the thought to the back of his mind, he let his host take back in control. He went to her memories. For the story we will use the name Tiffany for this host.

Apophis saw that Tiffany was a woman of status and she inherited a large sum of money from her parents who tragically passed three years ago in a shipwreck on their leisure cruise somewhere in the Atlantic Ocean. Tiffany had received word on the accident three days after the incident. It was believed that the ship was struck by a cannonball and sank, believing it was an enemy vessel.

Apophis also saw that Tiffany was a witch in secret because she could not openly worship for the fear of being killed the burning times were just 200 years before now and she worshipped Bastet. When he learned this, he quickly got annoyed.

Bastet appeared to Apophis right as he learned that his host was her worshipper.

"Hello, Apophis." Bastet said standing in front of Apophis.

"I had to be in a follower of yours, was it the Council's choice or yours?" Apophis said with annoyance in his voice.

Bastet remained silent with a glassy look in her eyes.

"Just as I figured, you can't tell me, a vow of silence on disclosing important information like that to the banished." Apophis said.

"Apophis, don't hurt this one, I see all my worshippers as children, and never harm a cat, they are my children as well." Bastet said.

Hello, it is me Bastet,

I am just popping in here to say, yes, all worshippers of me are my children and so are all the cats of this world. I am rather very disappointed in all of you. You have harmed many of the cats that come live with me. Why are you harming them? Cats are useful, they kill your pests such as snakes, rats and some bugs. Cats are loyal companions just like dogs. Cats are beautiful creatures. If you see a cat walking by or a kitten that is lost help them. -Bastet, Goddess and Mother of cats.

After telling Apophis that, Bastet turned and disappeared. Apophis went to the back of his host's mind, but still could peer through her eyes.

Tiffany was back in control of her own body, but she felt a bit off and she felt Apophis peering through her eyes. She walked over to the mirror and stared into the mirror.

"I know you are peering from behind my eyes, who are you?" Tiffany asked out loud with no one else around.

Apophis was shocked at first how Tiffany could sense him there, but then he remembered that she is a witch a very powerful witch that she was open with all her normal and sixth senses.

Apophis answered her normally inside her head like a normal person. He explained that he was known as Apophis the Egyptian demon, but not a bad demon. He explained that he was banished for one thousand years, by a group of all gods of every pantheon known as the council.

Of course, Tiffany was scared at first thinking she was mentally ill, she tried to understand but the human thinking of the time was limited, and Tiffany committed herself to a mental hospital. Apophis was shocked that a witch of this time period allowed her mind to be taken over with the beliefs of the time period. Could Tiffany really be called a Witch, if she couldn't handle a higher being speaking to her?

When Tiffany arrived at the local state mental hospital, there was a nurse at the reception desk.

"How many I help you mama? Are you visiting someone?" the nurse said.

"No, I am here to admit myself. I am hearing voices in my head." Tiffany said.

Wait, before we continue with the rest of the story here, I just want to interject that the experience you are about to read about is very traumatic. Mental hospitals at the time were not very regulated and there were a series of rapes and abuse within those hospitals. I must warn you; this host didn't fair well for being a female of the time in a mental hospital. -Apophis

The nurse stood up from her seat at her desk.

"Just one moment, please have a seat, I will have two of our nurses be right with you." The nurse said as she disappeared behind a door behind her desk.

About ten minutes later, the nurse came back with two tall men about six feet tall a piece. The had a white jacket with them that had the arms backwards and straps.

The two men grabbed and held Tiffany down, while they placed the jacket known as a "straight jacket" on her. Tiffany screamed and tried to fight back, but she was unable to stop them.

The nurse brought a wheelchair to put Tiffany in. The two men roughly forced Tiffany into the chair. Tiffany was trying to get loose from the straight jacket, but her efforts were useless. Apophis felt guilty that it was his fault for tiffany being in the mental hospital. The two men took Tiffany down a dimly lit hallway, when they reach a door number "16634". They unlocked the door and wheeled Tiffany into the room. The room was a small 12 foot by 6-foot room with nothing in the room but a mattress on the floor.

The two men lifted Tiffany off the wheelchair and laid her on the mattress. When they laid her on the bed, the two men whispered to one another, and both shook their heads. With Tiffany still in the straight jacket, the two men lifted Tiffany's dress and pulled down her underwear. Tiffany to fight back but the other man held her still while his partner raped Tiffany. Apophis never felt a penis inside him before, the connection with this host was strange. The feeling of the penis was something long, hard and, and a bit wide. Apophis felt the man finish inside his host's body. It was hot and dripping out from Tiffany's vagina.

When The man finished, he got up, pulled his pants up and let his partner have his way with Tiffany while he is holding Tiffany down. The same thing, Apophis felt him finish inside Tiffany's vagina as well.

Tiffany was on the verge of tears from being violated and raped. When the two men were done having their way with Tiffany, they went to the door, shut off the light and shut the door. Tiffany was crying by this point in the dark, she felt the semen inside her from both men. The semen was dripping out onto the bed as well. The stench of the Semen was horrendous, Smelling like bleach and cheese as well.

Apophis had never been raped before; he was shocked at how things went. As well how uncomfortable it was when the men forced their way in. Apophis knew this banishment was going to be a long process and this experience was just one of many.

The rest of the night, Tiffany couldn't sleep well with her arms bound in the straight jacket. She was tossing and turning all night long and crying most of the night.

It was about 3am when a female nurse walked in, her features couldn't be made of because it was dark in the room and the light from the hall was illuminating her back but making her front dark unable to see it. The nurse walked up to Tiffany, who was laying on the bed. The nurse crouched down to where she was at face level with Tiffany, but tiffany couldn't wake up, all she saw was a blur, Apophis left the body for just a moment to see what was going on. The nurse kissed Tiffany on the neck, even though Apophis was out of the body he could still feel it. The nurse was fondling Tiffany's breasts as he moved down to Tiffany's Vagina and began to finger it.

After twenty minutes the nurse removed her panties and rubbed her vagina on Tiffany's face and then against Tiffany's Vagina. All while this was happening Tiffany was barely conscious for this. Apophis witnessed the whole thing. The nurse even ate out Tiffany's vagina as well.

When the nurse finished, she pulled her panties back up and wiped her mouth on the sleeves of the straight jacket. She got up and turned and closed the door.

Apophis was shocked that a woman would rape another woman as well. He never knew such as thing before. All of this was new to him. He tried to sleep that night in the back of Tiffany's mind.

The next morning around 6a.m. the doctor walked in with a clipboard in his hand. He examined his clipboard for a moment.

"Time to awaken, Tiffany you are on the schedule for a special new experimental therapy session." The doctor said.

Tiffany still groggy, stumbled to the doctor. The doctor noticed that Tiffany was a mess. He motioned towards the nurse that was with him, it was a different nurse than the one from the previous night.

"Nurse, could you take tiffany and clean her up properly and get her a gown and shower and back in a clean straight jacket. Those damn fools from night shift can't do intakes well. They are supposed to bath the patients first before admitting them." The doctor said, ignoring the fact there was semen on Tiffany's leg.

The nurse that was with the doctor, led Tiffany to the shower area, she stripped Tiffany down and put her in the shower, she pulled out a bar of soap and turned the water on, the water was warm, and she began to bath Tiffany. There was a policy at this hospital for the nurses to bath the patients themselves, they don't trust the mentally sick patients to bath themselves.

The nurse was very attentive with Tiffany, she cleaned every inch of Tiffany's body very well. Tiffany didn't fight, she quite enjoyed being bathed, she was still half asleep. Apophis felt the experience was quite enjoyable as well.

After the nurse was done bathing Tiffany, she pulled some towels out from a closet that was in the restroom and dried Tiffany. She helped Tiffany into the gown and the straight jacket was firmly secured again onto Tiffany.

Tiffany frowned at the fact she now must wear a straight jacket for the rest of the remainder of her time there, she didn't know how long that would be.

After the shower, Tiffany was sat in a wheelchair, the nurse wheeled Tiffany down the long hall towards a room that was labeled "procedure". Tiffany was worried what procedure would they do to her. The nurse wheeled her in the room, she was lifted onto a bed by two different men. Straps were placed across her body and securely fastened.

The doctor had the hospital barber shave Tiffany's head completely bald. Once finished the doctor grabbed a hand crack drill and began to drill into Tiffany's skull. Tiffany screamed in pain; the pain was severe. Tears were coming out of Tiffany's eyes, the nurse quickly gagged Tiffany's mouth to silence her screams.

Apophis felt the sharp pain in his head as well. He realized that this doctor believed much like most primitive people of this time that this procedure would exile a demon from a body. However, in this case, Apophis cannot be removed this way or exorcism, he is not there by choice. The council put him there to punish him. So, far their plan is working, he was learning a whole new experience by being in a human body.

After three holes being drilled in Tiffany's skull, she had passed out from the trauma and pain.

Moments later when Tiffany regained consciousness, she reacted up and felt the top of her head, there was bandages on top of her head wrapped around. She was again back in her room, laying on the mattress that was on the floor in the room.

Apophis was amazed how the treatment went; he couldn't believe how primitive this society is acting. The Council never truly didn't want the human race their toys to advance in the first place.

After a few weeks, the same thing happened everyday of the drilling in the head, and every member of the staff would rape Tiffany each night. When it came time for Tiffany's period, it didn't come. Apophis sensed that his host was pregnant. The doctor was going to do bloodletting treatment, but he realized that Tiffany's body was forming a small medium sized baby bump.

The doctor ordered a blood test to confirm that Tiffany was pregnant. When the tests came back, he quickly had Tiffany sent to the maternity ward in a pad room there so she would not damage herself or the child. When she was placed in the room, the straight jacket was removed. Tiffany's arms were extremely sore to the point to where it was difficult to move them. Apophis knew this life wouldn't be good for the child. He decided to convince Tiffany to act viciously, kicking, screaming, scratching, and biting. He convinced her to do that to make sure the child doesn't end up in an orphanage.

The nurse walked in and

Tiffany ran at her and started punching her and screaming loudly. Two men came rushing in to subdue her, but Tiffany was biting, scratching, spitting, kicking and screaming. The men carried here down the hall as she was screaming to the procedure room. The doctor walked in as they were strapping her down.

"Well, Tiffany, I'm going to need to do a lobotomy on you to try and curb your aggression, I hope it doesn't harm your child." The doctor said walking behind Tiffany.

The doctor took his hand drill and began drilling into Tiffany's head and then he took his bone saw, cut a large chunk of skull off, but he cut way too deep, and Tiffany began bleeding uncontrollably. Apophis felt his host dying. His head was hurting he felt a tremendous pain.

Moments later, Apophis was back in the Eternal Blackness. He was still feeling the effect from the surgery. Bastet appeared out of the darkness.

"I am disappointed in you; you are responsible for her death. As well as leading her to the mental facility." Bastet said.

"I had to do it, the child would have ended up in an orphanage and the mother would have died either way, with or without my help." Apophis defended himself by pleading his case.

Bastet wasn't sure what else to say, she just looked at Apophis, then turned and disappeared into the blackness. Apophis just floated there. Waiting in the Eternal Blackness, is the true solitary confinement.

Unknown host #3

Apophis was floating and thinking in the Eternal Blackness, that is all you can do with no one around in the Eternal Blackness, is to be alone with your thoughts. Apophis thought on how he could get his revenge on the Council. He wandered what he could do to stop them and put an end to their reign once and for all.

Moments later, Apophis was encompassed by the same bright light as before, when he was transported to his last host. He awoken in a small shed like home, he was laying on a cotton stuffed mattress that had stains on it. He examined the clothes he was wearing and saw they were a bit worn down. Apophis got off the bed and went to the door that looked a bit worn down as well.

Once outside, Apophis saw a field of cotton stretching for a great distance as far as the eye could see. Apophis saw others dressed as him, worn out clothes. Apophis was confused on why the people looked exhausted and had scars on them. As well why were their white people carrying whips and guns. Apophis went up to one of them to ask when year it was, he was met with the butt of a gun to the face.

"Boy, why does it matter to you what year it is? Go back to the field and pick your cotton like a good boy or you will be lynched for your disobedience." The white gentleman commanded with hatred in his voice.

"Why don't you have respect for your fellow man, I am like you, a person." Apophis said.

Once Apophis said that he was met with another hit from the butt of the gun, he fell to the ground from the hit to the face, then the white gentleman kicked Apophis's host right in the stomach when he was on the ground.

"You are a Black slave; you are not like me. You are not a human." The white gentleman said.

Okay, before we continue to the rest of this host's story, I will not say the N-word for I do not want to offend anyone, so I will clean up the language and say things differently. -Apophis.

Apophis still feeling the sheer pain in the face and the stomach area, stood up to the gentleman, Apophis mustered all the energy he could into his host's right arm and punched the white gentleman right in the face, causing the gentleman to fell and pass out. Six other gentlemen came rushing over to subdue Apophis's host. One of them knocked Apophis over the head and Apophis blacked out.

When Apophis awoke still in control of the host's body, for the sake of the story we will name this host George. Apophis saw a young white woman with fancy dress and brunette hair. She has ice blue eyes, unique eyes.

"George, I had to persuade my father from killing you, you know that you cannot raise a hand against any of my father's foremen." The young woman said getting a wet washcloth from a bucket of water.

Apophis could sense that this young girl had a thing for his host, this could only lead to trouble, but he knew he could use this to his advantage.

"I apologize, I was just asking what year it was and he refused to tell me." Apophis said pretending to be the host.

"Well, the year is 1823, remember? You are also in my father's cotton plantation in Georgia." The young girl said.

"Thank you, Miss." Apophis said.

"I told you before you can call me Laura." Laura said kissing Apophis's forehead.

"Okay, Laura." Apophis said.

"I must go back, rest for another few minutes then come outside they will be serving food shortly." Laura said standing up and leaving the little hut.

Apophis got up from the very uncomfortable bed, felt much stronger now. He stepped out of the hut, he walked towards the main house when he saw the main owner of the house. He went to hide off somewhere so he could listen in on the conversation the owner was having with an associate.

"Halloween is almost here, Fredrick. How are the decoration? Is the guest list ready for tomorrow night's Halloween ball?" The owner said to his associate.

"Yes, sir. The decorations are almost ready and the invitations for those on the guest list have been sent out." Fredrick said.

"Good, I'll need a few of the slaves to help serve at the party tomorrow night, get some to volunteer to work for a few extra pieces of bread and meat." The owner said.

"Okay, sir. I'll get right on that." Fredrick said excusing himself from the owner of the property to carry out his orders.

Apophis heard the whole conversation. He had a cold chill run down his spine, Halloween. He knew his kids would find him and hurt him again. Apophis walked out from his hiding spot and went towards the foremen that he had an issue with earlier in the day.

"Excuse me, sir." Apophis said.

"What is it? Boy." The foreman said with aggression in his voice.

"I want to apologize for earlier, sir." Apophis said.

"Apologize? Don't you know your black apologizes have no meaning." The foreman said insulting Apophis.

Apophis tried to keep from letting his rage get ahold of him.

"Sir, I would you like to inform the owner's assistant Mr. Fredrick, that I want to serve at the Halloween party tomorrow night. If you do this for me, I will pick double the cotton next month." Apophis bargained.

The foreman laughed and called his other foremen buddies over.

"Hey, guys, this Boy, here is bargaining with me to put in a good word for him to the boss's assistant to serve at the Boss's Halloween party tomorrow night!" The foreman shouted all around and laughing at this requested.

The other foreman came walking up to see what the one foreman was laughing at.

With everyone starting to gather around Apophis and the foremen, the owner caught wind of it and was heading down to the spot where everyone was encircling Apophis and the foreman. When he arrived, he heard the foreman shouting about how ridiculous the request was that the slave made.

"Well, I think his request to serve at the party tomorrow night is a swell idea indeed." The boss said.

The foremen quickly got back into his professional façade.

"Hello, boss, I'm sorry, but I believe this boy is unfit to serve at the party." The foreman lied.

"George is a bad worker, he *will* by my order serve at the party tomorrow night, do you understand Franklin?" the boss said firmly.

The foreman complied and went back to work with great embarrassment. Apophis chuckled on the inside of his mind at the sight of the foreman being embarrassed by the boss. The boss walked up to Apophis.

"Come here, George." The owner said welcoming him warmly.

Apophis walked up to the boss.

"Yes, sir?" Apophis said.

"I am glad you stood up for yourself earlier today but be careful these guys feel you are like a bug on their boot that needs to be scraped off." The boss said.

The boss didn't see his slaves as property at all, he saw them as equals mostly, but for the sake of status and economical class he had to treat his slaves like slaves as a show for the most part.

"Thank you, Sir for the advice. I will try to keep out of their way." Apophis said.

"Good, Now I would love to have you serve at the Halloween party tomorrow night. We will need to get you washed and dressed nicely before the party tomorrow night. I will send one of the other servants to fetch you tomorrow about three hours before the party." The boss said.

"Yes, sir. Thank you for giving me this chance." Apophis said.

After the conversation, the owner went back to the main house as Apophis went to go work the field a bit before mealtime. The sun was beating down on him, Apophis let his host take back control to do the physical work. Apophis didn't like physical work, he went to the back of George's mind, which was surprisingly empty. He only had a limited mind because he wasn't taught to have his own mind. Apophis knew he would be bored in the mind.

Bastet appeared to Apophis; she had the expression of disappointment on her face.

"What is it feline?" Apophis asked.

"You are breaking rules, you are not supposed to manipulate people during your banishment, the Council has called a hearing for you." Bastet said warning Apophis.

"When is thi..." before Apophis could finish his sentence, he was transported to the council chamber, standing in the middle of the chamber.

RA stepped out on the balcony just above Apophis. He stared down and shouted "Apophis you have broken several rules that you were not supposed to break. Your banishment will be extended another 2,000 years." RA declared.

Apophis felt a rage form behind his eyes as a burning feeling. Apophis was about to shout at RA to defend himself, but RA had already sent him back to his current host.

When Apophis got back to his host, it was at night, the Halloween party was 30 minutes away. Apophis was inside the main house in the kitchen, Laura the boss's daughter came up to Apophis.

"George, there is something I need your help with upstairs." Laura said in a tone that Apophis identified as flirting.

"What is it that you need help with Miss Laura?" Apophis said.

Laura took Apophis's hand and started to lead him up the stairs that were in the kitchen.

"I will show you." Laura said firmly gripping Apophis's hand.

As Apophis and Laura walked to the top of the stairs, Laura went down the hall with Apophis until they came to a set of double French doors. Laura opened the doors and lead Apophis into the room. She shut the doors behind him and locked them.

"What was it that you needed help with?" Apophis said turning to face Laura.

Laura looked at Apophis in the face as she started to undo her large fancy dress of the time.

"I have been dreaming of you doing me hard in my bed." Laura said with a deep lustful look in her eyes.

"Laura, I can't have sexual relations with you." Apophis said.

Laura was fully nude at this point, her breasts were young and firm, her body was skinny and lovely round buttocks. She walked up to Apophis and began to undo his clothes. Apophis tried to stop her, but she reached into his pants a squeezed his cock and balls hard, harder than Apophis had ever felt before.

"You will have sexual relations with me, or I will have you lick one of the dog's asses" Laura threaten.

Apophis complied with Laura's demands, when he was fully nude, Laura had him lay down on the bed as she got on top of him. She stuck the seven-inch cock inside her. When she did this, she let out a loud moan. She began to thrust in different rhythms.

Meanwhile, downstairs in the kitchen the boss was looking for George, when one of the other servants told him that he went with Laura to her room. He started to get in raged. He got three of his foremen, some guns and a rope for a hanging. The boss and his three men stormed up the stairs.

When they got to Laura's room door, they could hear her moaning and enjoying herself. They tried to open the door.

"Laura, stop what you are doing, you are sinning, we are going to bust this door down." The boss said busting the doors down.

The boss saw his own daughter naked in bed with one of his slaves, on top of him. The boss walked up to his daughter and slapped her across the face hard enough to cause her to fall back on to the bed. Once he did that, he grabbed Apophis by to the neck and dragged him out into the front of the yard. Apophis's host was still naked.

When Apophis and the boss, as well as the rest of the foremen were outside, he was pushed to the ground.

"You did wrong boy; you will be hung for this." The boss said with anger in his voice.

Apophis stood up, when he did, he saw his 2,000 children standing next to the boss and the foremen.

"What are you staring at, boy?" The foremen said looking around unable to see Apophis's children.

"Nothing." Apophis said.

One of the foremen tossed the hanging rope over the tree and situated the noose around Apophis's neck. Apophis's kids just stood there like ghosts watching the torment Apophis was about to experience.

"On the count of three, I want you three strong men to pull the rope, lifting George off the ground and tie it off to that tree there, it is the strongest to hold his weight." The boss commanded his foremen.

The three foremen went to the other side of the tree, they each grabbed the rope.

"Any last words?" The boss said.

"You will fail, your racism will fail" Apophis said.

The boss raised his arm and dropped it indicating for his foremen to pull.

Apophis was lifted off the ground and felt the rope tighten around his throat, he was suffocating.

Within a matter of moments, Apophis was back in the Eternal Blackness. He was floating there, still feeling the effects of the noose around his neck.

Unknown host #4

Apophis floated there in the Eternal Blackness; he wandered why the Council put hard rules to follow. He knew none of them from the council especially since none of them could control their urges to manipulate humans and of course their sexual appetites, especially RA's sexual appetite. He has had millions of women in his lifetime. There is no way he could follow the rules that he is forcing on Apophis.

Moments later, Apophis was encompassed by the bright light, he was transported into a new host that was in man in a position of power, a congressman. Apophis got up from the chair that the congressman fell asleep into. Apophis walked over to the desk in the room he was in. He saw a calendar that said he was in the year 1825.

Apophis shuffled through paper on the desk of his new host to try and find out more about this point in history. Apophis found many papers on wanting to expand further west further than the land that was purchased 22 years ago, known as the *Louisiana Purchase*. There were documents of land purchase for this congressman. He was getting royalties from the coastal land purchase in the territory of the *Louisiana Purchase*. For the sake of the story, we will name this host Rupert. Apophis bumped into a cabinet below the desk. Apophis crouched down in front of it, he opened it and saw that the cabinet was full of alcohol, mostly whiskey. Apophis took a bottle of the whiskey, stood up and grabbed a cup and poured him some. He wondered what it tasted like, his last three hosts never drank alcohol. Also, back in his time there was beer and wine.

Apophis took a sip and he had never tasted something so spicy and dry; he spit it out and put the bottle back.

"What an awful tasting invention these humans have made." Apophis said out loud to himself.

"Well, of course it is, they can't mix things together to make them taste good." A voice said from behind Apophis.

Apophis turned to see who it was, his eyes nearly popped out of his head when he saw Anubis standing behind him. Anubis, the jackal headed Egyptian god of mummification and death. He stood proud behind Apophis, his ears were pointed as if they were standing on guard, as if they are making sure no one is sneaking up on him, his long snout pointed outward, his physical body was that of a human, muscular with a tail coming out the back.

"What are you doing here?" Apophis asked.

"I am here to see how your banishment is, I also wanted to inform you, I will be watching for the moment, Bastet is indisposed at the moment." Anubis said.

"What is her cat collection still growing?" Apophis said being cynical in his tone of voice.

"Yes, but it is more of her children not a collection, she must look after them after death." Anubis said correcting Apophis.

"Look I am busy here, could you just go and go guide the dead to the underworld or something, thanks puppy." Apophis mocked Anubis.

Anubis got irritated from the mocking comment Apophis had made. Anubis turned to leave without saying another word to Apophis. Apophis continued to learn more about his host, then came a knock at the door. Apophis went to the front door and opened it. At the door was a child selling newspaper.

"Hello, sir. I am selling today's paper; would you like one?" the child said holding up the newspaper.

"Yes, I would love one, how much?" Apophis asked pulling out a dollar from his host's pocket.

"Ten cents, sir." The child said.

Apophis handed the child the dollar in his host's pocket and took the paper, before the child could give Apophis his change, he stopped the child and told his to keep the change, and that he would need the money more than him.

The child was shocked and happy while he looked as if he was on the verge of tears. He hugged Apophis and thanked Apophis, the child turned and left.

Apophis went back inside the house and sat in a chair, he let his host take back in control.

Rupert was shocked that he was still at home until 2pm in the afternoon, of course this wasn't the first time, he has had a lot of drunken hangovers to where he slept longer and missed congress's meeting. He put his shoes on and went down to the local brothel to pick up a woman. On his way to the brothel, a gang of men that were mad at congress, and money hungry, they jumped Rupert, stabbing him repeatedly, Apophis felt every knife entry. Within a blink of an eye, Apophis was back in the Eternal Blackness.

Apophis was shocked to see that he was in a short-lived host. He shouted in anguish into the Eternal Blackness, but there was no echo. Apophis stopped shouting after ten minutes, he was starting to go crazy in the Eternal Darkness, but he knows he must not show that he wants to give up, for if he did, that would be signing his death certificate with the Council.

Unknown host #5

Apophis floated there in the Eternal Darkness, his ever-growing boredom was getting to the point of annoyance, until Apophis was engulfed in the light again.

Apophis awoke in a home of a 1,000-pound host. He couldn't move because of the weight. This host was being washed by a cloth and bucket from a woman that lived with the host. An advisor walked into the room.

"Sir, as leader of our village, I have brought you the best of the food in the village." The advisor said.

The advisor called in some servant girls to bring in plates of the finest meats, fish, and crops from the village farmers. Apophis was amazed at how much food there was, he hadn't seen such a feast since he had his own servants. Apophis picked up the meat with his hand and devoured it in front of the advisor.

"My lord, some important information for you, your magician has arrived." The advisor said ushering in the magician.

The magician walked into the large room. He was a thin gentleman with a bag of potions.

"My lord, you summoned me?" the magician said.

Apophis let his host have control again, Apophis went to the memories to learn that the host had many appetites he loved food, women and wishing for immortality. The Magician was tasked in finding the secret of immortality for the host. For the purpose of the story, we will call him Tzu, and the magician we will call Wang.

"I want you to research an elixir to help me to live forever, you will have 6 months to figure this out, and you will be richly rewarded with 200,000 gold coins." Tzu said.

"As you wish, my lord." Wang said walked out of the room.

Apophis laughed at the foolish host, he knew it was 1828, Apophis knew he could easily manipulate both the host and the magician. Apophis was disgusted at the host that he was in. Apophis left his hosts body temporarily, but not permanently because he was still attached to the host's body. Apophis did a sort of out of body experience. He left the body while his host slept to go find Wang.

When Apophis had located Wang, Wang was meditating, Apophis slipped into his meditation session.

"Wang, I am the great spirit that knows everything that there is to be known. What do you seek to know?" Apophis said fooling the human.

"Yes, oh great one, I seek the recipe for an immortality elixir, do you know this?" Wang said bowing before Apophis who had shapeshifted into a great serpent before the eyes of Wang.

"Yes, I do, listen to my words closely." Apophis said.

"Yes, I will, oh great one, I am your humble servant, bless me with your knowledge." Wang said.

Apophis started to let the appraisals from wang go to his head, like a dopamine rush, he missed the euphoria from being worshipped like he was so many thousands of years ago.

"Go to the mountain with liquid mercury, mix it with the blood of three virgins, as well as the gold of the honey dew flower, mix and drink it in a bowl not a cup." Apophis said knowing that the amount of mercury would surely kill his host and he would not have to suffer in the fat blob. He is vain when it comes to the image of his hosts. Vanity is a trait that all the Gods and Goddess hold, especially those in the Council. The only reason humans think vanity is a sin is because the Council did not want humans to have that trait, so they implanted the idea into a Christian leader so many centuries ago that it was a sin.

Okay, let me explain, the Council has created all your world religions to cause you harm not good. Christianity, Judaism, Islam, and many others. These were created to cause chaos; the Council finds enjoyment of you guys hurting each other for "religious" reasons. They created your "seven deadly sins" to cause you pain and suffering to entertain them not to advance you. -Apophis.

"Thank you, Oh great one." Wang said as Apophis departed back to his host's body.

The magician took three weeks of a journey to collect the ingredients for the elixir. While the magician was collecting the ingredients, Apophis was directing the servants and soldiers to do Apophis's bidding. He ordered the soldiers that were sworn to protect the village to attack neighboring villages and assimilate their people and resources into his own to expand the village into a grand empire.

Apophis periodically checked on the magician's progress. The place Wang stopped was a pool of mercury in the secret sacred mountains, he collected a gallon of the liquid mercury. He went on to the sacred forest which the golden honey dew grew, when he located a patch of golden honey dew flowers, he collected the nectar of each flower giving him about half a gallon worth of sacred nectar. He then went to the nearest village and paid each of the three families handsomely to collect a pint of virgin blood from each of the daughter of the families.

Apophis watched as Wang collected each of these items, he didn't do an out of body experience though, he did a form of scrying to see long distances. Apophis was happy with what he saw of Wang's progress, Bastet saw as well and was highly disappointed with Apophis, she couldn't believe Apophis would go to such a low level to kill his host because he was unhappy in the host body because of a weight issue, however she thought to herself, is she so different? She wouldn't have wanted to be trapped in a large overweight host, if she was in his position. Bastet knew none of the other Gods and Goddess would have let an overweight host live as well, so she would let this one pass.

Three days later, Wang returned to the village and went up to the leader's house. He went up to the leader of the village with the finished elixir.

"My lord, I have consulted with the spirits, and they have given me a recipe for immortality elixir." Wang said holding the bowl of the mercury with the other ingredients in it.

Tzu's eyes grew large, like a child in a candy shop at the sight of the elixir. Tzu took the bowel and began to guzzle it down as fast as he could with no concern about the taste. Once he finished the bowel of elixir, he looked at Wang.

"You have done well, as promised your gold is ready." Tzu said motioning for his servants to bring the gold coins.

A few minutes after Tzu's stomach started to degrade from the mercury, he grabbed his belly and began to become very nauseated and vomiting up blood, he was having heart issues as well, withing moments, Apophis was back in the Eternal Blackness.

Bastet appeared to Apophis as he floated in the Eternal Blackness. She had the look of disappointment on her face.

"How could you have killed that host for selfish reasons?" Bastet scolded.

"Oh, don't act all high and mighty, I know you would have done the same thing if you were in my position. I had to get out of that fat lard, he gave me the perfect opportunity." Apophis said with a grin upon his face.

"The Council will used that against you." Bastet said.

"I know this, but I know they would have done the same if they were banished like me, I will used that against them." Apophis said all full of himself.

Bastet remained silent and stared at Apophis for a moment.

Unknown host #6

Moments without warning during Apophis and Bastet's conversation, Apophis was thrown violently into a new host, Apophis had awoken in a host that was in a ship's cabin. Apophis stood up off the bed, that he was laying on, he went to a small trunk that was on the floor, he opened it. Apophis saw letters from the host's family and wife from America. He learned the year was 1830.

Apophis closed the trunk, and then stepped out of the cabin, for the rest of the story we will call this host Jack. He is a commander of the vessel, turns out the vessel was a Navy vessel. The ship was on its way to Egypt, the ship was already on the west coast of Africa.

Apophis was shocked to be so close to Egypt once again, his home. Apophis took control and looked out over the Atlantic Ocean. The smell of the Atlantic has not changed, it brought a tear to Apophis's eyes. He missed the travel and his time.

The memories of my time period, I have travelled all over the world back in my time, I have seen all the cultures of this world evolve and change as well as fall. I know how things were and the rest of the Council has seen the same, they have seen dinosaurs of course, but they didn't see any value of a dinosaur. Humans can give them the power and gratifications they crave. As well they take the essence you give them, and they use it to get strength. -Apophis

Apophis was three days away from Cairo, Egypt. Apophis was taking in the sights of the ocean water; he had wished that he didn't have to travel like this back to his original home. Egypt would always be in his blood and his memory.

Back in his day, the ocean waters were more tamed than they are now, men prayed to their Gods to keep the waters calm for their travel and some did listen to their followers, but if the Council got bored of being the Gods that they are, they sent disasters to entertain themselves and they loved watching Mankind grovel on their knees for protection.

Much like today, mankind has not changed, they still ask a "God" for help.

Apophis knew the council had something to do with all world religions. He wandered how much further things would be in the future.

As Apophis watched as the sunset in the distance, a crewmen came up on the deck from down below.

"Commander, the meal is ready in the mess hall." The crewmember said.

"I'll be there in a few minutes." Apophis said moving away from the ship railing and walking towards the door.

When Apophis arrived at the mess hall, there was a long table with assorted foods that were stored on board, enough to feed 3,000 men. Apophis took a seat at the table. There was a plate of three-inch-thick steaks. Apophis grabbed three of the steaks, there were steamed potatoes, fancy wine, the best wine of the time. There were three cakes, in three flavors, vanilla, chocolate and regular grain cake.

The crewmen were feasting on the food, there was even a plate of ribs. Apophis hoped that meals like this came to him with almost every host during this banishment. It would make this banishment more enjoyable, but Apophis didn't know what was in store for him with future hosts.

"So, Commander, what do you plan to do in Egypt?" a private asked the commander.

"Well, I was ordered to give everyone three days of R and R, when we get there." Apophis said knowing he had learned that from his hosts memory.

All the crewmembers raised their glasses in excitement.

After dinner, Apophis's went back to the commander's quarters, when he got back in the quarters, he was going through the small desk the was in the room, he found a log of everything that his host had desired. This log wasn't a navy issued log, more like a personal journal of his host. There were signs of rage against the leader of the country, the commander desired to murder the president of the country because he believed that the president was abusing his political power. He even wanted to be president in away to fix the issues of the presidency, such as the lack of respect the president was giving the people. This host's family were living in a rundown home that wasn't very good, but it was the best the military budget could buy.

"You know you are in the host to learn humility, not take advantage of the host's power." Bastet said standing behind Apophis while he was reading the personal journal of the host.

Apophis turned to face Bastet. He looked her dead in the eye.

"I can do as I please, go away Bastet." Apophis said full of himself.

"So be it, you are making a mistake." Bastet said warning Apophis.

"Shut up." Apophis said.

Enraged Bastet pushed Apophis into his hosts mind, not allowing him to regain control of the host again, only to watch. This in turn pissed Apophis off, but he was helpless to fight against Bastet, he was not at his full power anymore, she was more powerful than him now.

Apophis watched as his host directed his crew to turn the ship into a coral reef. The ship was badly damaged, but the commander tried to get his crew to push on and keep moving but the ship was beginning to sink. The commander was overconfident that his ship was still in working order even though it was sinking. With in moments the ship with her commander and crew were below the ocean. Apophis was back in the Eternal Elackness again, he had tasted the cold salt water in his mouth, even with him in the eternal darkness. Bastet appeared into the eternal darkness in front of Apophis. Her face was heavy with disappointment.

"I could have prevented those deaths." Apophis pleaded to Bastet.

"No, you were caught up in your own selfish endeavor, those men were necessary sacrifices." Bastet said wiping her tail about.

Unknown host # 7

Apophis and Bastet were sitting there in the Eternal Darkness, Bastet didn't have much else to say to Apophis, she turned and left Apophis alone. Apophis was engulfed in the light again shortly after Bastet had turned to leave.

Apophis had awoken in another bedroom. This bedroom was plain, there was an older looking dresser in the corner of the room. Apophis got up, he looked around the room, he saw he was dressed in a plain shirt with overalls. Apophis went out of the room to the kitchen. Apophis saw in the kitchen was a beautiful woman with blonde hair and a pretty blue dress on, she was busy making bacon and eggs for breakfast, sitting at the table was a little 5 year old girl, she had blonde hair as well.

"Good morning, papa." The little girl said swinging her legs at the table.

"Good morning, dear." Apophis said sitting at the table.

For the rest of this story, we will call the host, John, the wife, Nancy and the daughter Emma.

"John, I'm going to take Emma to school, and then go shopping in town for a new broom and new hairbrush, do you need anything?" Nancy said putting down the morning paper and a plate of food in front of him.

"No, I don't need anything." Apophis said opening the paper. Apophis saw that the date was 1832, and that the location was in Oklahoma.

Apophis figured that he was in a farmer, since he saw the crops outside. Apophis looked at the plate and began to eat the food. While he was eating, he suddenly was pushed into the hosts mind, letting the host take control again.

Bastet was standing the back of the host's mind. Bastet had a cold look on her face.

"What is it, Bastet?" Apophis said confused.

"I have come to tell you a bit about your current host. He and his family are one of many families that this newly formed government had offered land to, in an expansion plan. This plot of land is worth $150,000 dollars that you are standing on." Bastet said.

"Wow, that isn't a bad value, are there any special resources on this land?" Apophis said.

"I will not disclose that with you, you are not to search either, you are to be getting punished not finding ways to make it rich." Bastet scolded.

"What else do I need to know about this host and family?" Apophis asked.

"Well, this host has a rage that needs to be controlled, he also has a suspension that his wife is cheating on him. His wife is in fact cheating on him, she has been for three years, she is unhappy being married to a farmer." Bastet said.

"Oh wow, I am not surprised there, she smelled like she was cheating, I smelled a scent on her." Apophis said.

Meanwhile, outside of the mind, John had heard what Nancy had said thanks to Bastet pulling Apophis to the back of the mind at the right moment.

"How much do you need, Nancy?" John said pulling out his wallet.

"$75 dollars." Nancy said

"$75 dollars?!" John exclaimed.

"No broom or hairbrush costs $75 dollars!" John shouted.

Nancy was enraged, she responded with a bit of irritation.

"Well, I might get our daughter something and might grab a bit to eat after dropping our daughter off to school, and I might find something that I want to surprise you with." Nancy said making John feel bad.

"Okay, I am sorry, I didn't realize." John said handing Nancy the money.

"Thank you, and that is right you don't realize much anyway, John." Nancy said insulting John.

"Well, I am going to nap a bit while you are gone, I love you, Nancy." John said feeling a bit guilty and irritation in his voice.

Nancy ignored John and didn't notice that he said that he loved her or the irritation in his voice.

A few minutes later, John hugged his daughter goodbye as her and Nancy left the house. John went to the bedroom upstairs for his mid-morning nap from his field work at his farm early in the morning. When Apophis had arrived in the body earlier, John was going to lay down for a nap then, but Apophis had taken control.

While John slept, Apophis did an out of body astral travel to spy on the wife. When Apophis had located her, she was completely naked and being pounded by a younger gentleman in his twenties. Nancy was moaning long and hard into the thrusts from the young gentleman. Apophis knew that if John were to find out, he would go insane. Apophis saw Nancy's face getting red from the enjoyment of having sexual encounters with the young strapping young man with brown hair. Apophis watched for a few minutes then went back to his host body.

Apophis knew that John is going to get enraged if he even tried to find out.

About two hours later, John had awoken from his nap, he got up off the bed to go fix something to eat in the kitchen, he felt hungry when he had awoken. John noticed that his wife had not returned home.

"Nancy? Are you home?" John shouted down the stairs, all he could hear was his voice echo off the walls of the empty house.

When John made his way into the kitchen, his thoughts were beginning to swarm like locusts. He felt anger and hatred stew within him. John went over to a cabinet by the kitchen sink, he opened it and there was a stash of jars of homemade moonshine. John grabbed a jar and opened it and began to drink it.

Within two hours, John had become extremely drunk from drinking the four jars of moonshine that fed into his rage. Apophis didn't like the feeling of the drunkenness. He couldn't even take control of the body to stop John from a self-destructive action.

On the second hour of drinking the moonshine, Nancy and Emma came home, Nancy saw the jar of moonshine, she quickly became frightened of John because she knew how he gets when he drinks. John turned to look at Nancy, when he saw her, he raised the empty moonshine jar above his head and preceded to walk towards Nancy.

"WHERE THE HELL WERE YOU? FUCKING WHORE?" John screamed in rage at Nancy with the jar above his head ready to attack Nancy with it.

Nancy froze in fear, but she did manage to say, "I WAS FUCKING A YOUNGER GUY THAN YOU, BECAUSE YOU ARE A WORTHLESS PIECE OF SHIT!!!" Nancy screamed at John still standing in one stop afraid to run or defend herself.

John got more enraged that he hit his daughter with the empty jar completely missing his intended target. The glass shattered across Emma's face she collapsed to the floor. John grabbed another jar and hit Nancy with it before she could do anything about the death of their daughter. Nancy fell to the ground with her face full of glass, her face was gushing in blood. John went to another cabinet and pulled out a cast iron pan.

John preceded to bash Nancy's face with the cast iron pan to ensure that she was dead. He did the same to their daughter to ensure she was dead as well.

Once he finished doing that, he went to the stove and pulled it out, broke the natural gas line, pulled out some matches, as well as the last bottle of moonshine. John went over to his dining table chair as he let the gas fill the house with a hissing sound, John took a long gulp of the moonshine before igniting the match that led to a large explosion.

Apophis was thrown into the Eternal Blackness with burning flesh, he felt the effects of the explosion still on his skin.

Apophis let out a huge scream of agony into the Eternal Darkness.

Unknown host #8

Apophis floated in the eternal darkness, he felt a rage build within him, he let out a loud scream into the Eternal Darkness. Apophis felt a burning grudge build within him towards the Council. He wished that they were not being petty and framing him for something that he did not commit. Apophis knew one day he would take his revenge upon the Council. Apophis was wishing this torment would end, the feeling of each death was traumatizing, each one fuels his rage.

Within a matter of moments that felt like thirty minutes, Apophis was engulfed in a bright light. Apophis had awoken at a desk in a large back room. Apophis looked around. He saw he had a shoe and a tool in his hand to work on shoes. Apophis set them both down on the desk and got up from the chair.

Apophis found a newspaper that was laying on a table in the backroom, Apophis picked it up, he saw the date was 1838, He was in England, city of London.

Apophis step to the front room and looked around the store, suddenly the front door opened. A lady walked into the store; she was in a blue dress that was a bit puffy. Apophis was surprised at how the fashion of this century was. For the purpose of this story, we will call this host Mr. North or just North.

"Mr. North, can you have my new shoes delivered by tomorrow?" the customer asked.

Apophis didn't know what to say so he went to the back of the mind to observe what was going on and to learn more about his host. Mr. North came back at the right moment to give a proper answer to the customer's question.

"Yes, but why not send your daughter to get them? I have other orders to fill as well by tomorrow as well." Mr. North said.

"Okay, I'll send a liaison tomorrow to pick up my order." The customer said turning to leave.

Apophis was going through the host's memories;

h e saw that the host was a well-respected person in the city of London, Apophis saw that Mr. North was one of the top shoe shops in the whole city, the elite of the city even come and visit him. He had a well-known business in this city. Apophis sensed a darker secret that he could not see, the host kept that well-hidden even from himself.

A gentleman that was well dressed walked into the shop; The gentleman was one of the rich elites. He was preparing for one of the best parties of the year. There were several throughout the year, but this one was a big blowout so to speak. Apophis saw North dreaming about joining the elite at the party one day. What confused Apophis was why hadn't North been able to join the elites, since he was well off just like them?

Turns out, North was never invited to their parties because they saw him as a lower-class citizen, they didn't want him there. The gentleman walked up to the counter, holding his hat under his arm.

"Mr. North, I would like you to create me a pair of leather shoes with gold and silver on the laces and heels, also if you have a ruby in stock, could you add that to it as well?" The gentleman said pulling out his wallet.

"That will be 650 shillings." North said.

"I will give you 200 shilling extra if you can get it done by tomorrow." The gentleman said putting out the shillings on the counter.

North rang up the gentleman, he wrote him up a receipt and handed it to him. North place the money in a heavy oak box with an iron pad lock on it that he kept under the counter.

Once North put the money away, he went to the door and locked it. He placed a closed sign on the door as well. Once he finished, he turned and went to the back room. He walked towards a door that was hidden in the corner of the room. This door had seven latches on it and a big pad lock as well, the same iron one that was on the oak box. North unlatched the latches and removed the padlock. When North opened the door, he took an oil lamp into the small little room that had stairs at the back out of about three feet away from the front door of the room, North walked towards the steps and began to descend down the stairs.

When he got to the bottom of the steps, he turned towards a large iron door that was about ten feet tall and ten feet wide, bank usually used for the safes. North walked up to it and began to put in his code on the combination lock, his heart began to quicken, Apophis felt uneasy on what was behind this door. Apophis felt that his host becoming aroused from what was behind the door.

Once the door was open, North stepped inside with the oil lamp in his hand. North put the oil lamp in front of him to see inside. The light from the oil lamp exposed a young blonde girl about the age of thirteen years old. Her hands and feet were bound with a rope, her eyes blindfolded, and her mouth gagged, she was sitting on a bench type seat with the middle cut out so she could go to the bathroom. There was a bucket at the bottom of the bench.

Upon further inspection of the young girl, she had her arms, legs and the rest of her body were bruised up, her dress was torn to shreds to the point that the dress was completely gone. Her hands were bound above her head. Apophis couldn't bear to see this poor child in this condition. The girl was merely 5 feet 4 inches tall, very pale skin.

North knelt in front of her to see if the bucket was full. He grabbed a bowl that was laying on the floor and a cup as well that was next to it. He reached in the bucket with the bowl and filled it will the feces. He stood up and opened his pants, pulling out his penis and urinated into the cup. North then went to the young girl at face level, removed the blindfold and the gag out of her mouth. The girl licked her dry lips. He touched her cheek gently.

"Are you hungry and thirsty, my pet?" North said with a sinister look on his face.

The young girl shook her head slowly and licked her dry lips again. North poured the cup of urine into her mouth and the young girl had no choice but to drink it, she was extremely thirsty. North then placed a spoonful of feces into her mouth. Apophis was disgusted at the sight of it, he was powerless to do anything. Apophis learned that this girl was fed like this for three months.

"Are you ready for your sweet treat, my pet?" North said before ramming is erect penis into the young girl's vagina.

The young girl let out an enormous scream in pain, North struck her across the face to shut her up as he continued the rape the poor child.

When North was close to finishing, he grabbed her hair and ejaculated inside the young girl. He pulled out still fully erect and shoved his penis into her mouth and shot his ejaculate into her mouth, when he finished, he quickly gagged her and blindfolded her once more.

North turned to leave the young girl there in the safe still gagged and bound, North shut the iron door to the room. North turned to go up the stairs, once he got to the top of the stairs he went through the door, latched and locked it.

North then went to his desk to begin work on the shoes.

Apophis was disgusted at what he saw, but he knew he was powerless to help her, he had to find a different way to help. Bastet Appeared to Apophis.

"You saw your host's dark secret?" Bastet said.

"Well, that is more of a disgusting dark secret than just a dark secret." Apophis said making a disgusted face.

Bastet just stared at Apophis with a neutral face.

"I thought you were a protector of children as well? Why would you let this happen to a child?" Apophis asked with a pointed question, knowing it hurts Bastet.

Bastet started to feel uneasy with the questions Apophis asked.

"I usually am, but the Council overrides my power and places these children in harms way. They have slaughtered millions of children already and they do this as an enjoyment, no one is safe with the Council in control." Bastet said feeling hurt by what she had said held true.

Yes, I must apologize for the darkness of this host, but I must write the events as I have seen them. All the pain that any victim has experienced was a result of the council. The Council believes humans are toys to them. They don't take care of their toys as you have read so far. I must warn you from here, the rest of the host's stories are not peaceful. -Apophis.

"I don't fear the council, unlike you, I am going to try and save her tonight." Apophis declared with confidence in his voice, knowing that this host would be killed soon.

"But you can't go against the rules, you cannot interfere with this event." Bastet protested.

"Screw the rules and screw the Council, it is wrong for them to put this innocent child in harms way for the sadistic pleasure of this maniac." Apophis said turning to observe what his host was doing.

Apophis saw that North was busy making the rich gentleman's shoes, he had almost finished them, the perception of time was much slower inside the Mindspace, in the real world three hours had passed. The shoes were almost complete, North was in the process of fitting the ruby stone onto the shoes.

Once he completed them, he placed them in a box, placed the customers receipt on the box and took the boxed-up shoes to the front and placed them on the counter. North returned to his desk and began to read a book, *The Wonders of Geology by Gideon Mantell*. North had an interest in geology as well. After 45 minutes of reading, North fell asleep.

Apophis took control of the body; Apophis felt a bit dazed as if he was in a drunken state because he could feel the exhaustion of the body. Apophis placed the book onto the desk. He got up from the chair that was situated at the desk. Apophis quickly rushed over to the door in the corner with the latches and lock. Apophis unlatched the door, but first he grabbed a knife from the desk, he was going to give the knife to the girl.

Once Apophis had the door open, he quickly rushed down the stairs and went towards the large iron door. Apophis opened the door with the code that he had seen North put in. He pulled the door open, he went to the girl and cut her hand and feet free from their bounds, he removed the gag and blindfold.

The girl collapsed to the floor, very weak from being bound for hours on end, Apophis caught her that way she could not completely hit the floor, he laid her on the floor gently. Apophis got her some clean water to drink, as well placed the knife next to her for when she had awoken. Apophis knew her body need time to recover. Apophis quickly left, leaving the door open so the girl could escape. Apophis made his way up the stairs, left the door unlatched. Apophis sat back at the desk and went back to sleep.

Meanwhile, down in the room that the girl was in, she had awoken in a cold sweat. She looked around and saw that she was no longer bound and that there was a clean bowl of water with a knife next to it. She looked towards where the door is and saw it was wide open. The girl took long gulps of water, before grabbing the knife. She stood up slowly still knowing she was still weak. The girl wabbled out of the room and slowly made her way up the stairs.

Once she got to the top of the stairs, she walked through the door quietly, when she made her way through the door, she saw North asleep at his desk, North was in a deep sleep.

The girl slowly crept up behind north, she saw his head laying on the desk, she slowly reached over to grab his hair, she quickly grabbed a hand full of hair and yanked it hard, she pulled back exposing his throat.

She screamed in his ear "ARE YOU READY FOR YOUR SWEET TREAT, BITCH!" the girl said slicing his throat with the knife.

The blood began to gush out, North awoke for a brief moment gasping for air, he reached up to his throat, pulled back his hand an saw a large amount of blood and began to panic, Apophis felt it and was on his way back to the eternal darkness.

<u>The Council summons again</u>

Apophis thought he was on the way to the Eternal Darkness, until he had appeared in the middle of the Council chamber. Apophis looked around confused on why he was brought to the Council chambers.

RA walked forward on to his high balcony with his body and beak glistening in the light that it made your eyes hurt when looking at him.

Apophis looked up at him and chuckled at how ridiculous RA looked.

"Apophis, you learned to save the life of an innocent life, but you are still punished for over a thousand years, possibly more thousands will be added to your sentence. Do you have anything to say?" RA roared down from his high balcony above Apophis.

"You assholes didn't summon me here to just tell me that now, did you?" Apophis challenge the Council.

The entire chamber started to grow loud with growls from every Council member growling at Apophis.

"You cowards! I will have my revenge upon you one day, I swear it!" Apophis yelled.

The growling turned into a loud hissing sound from every member of the Council. Apophis was sent away into the Eternal Darkness. Apophis felt his anger and rage build stronger within him.

The Cycle Continues

Uknown host #9

Apophis had awoken to find himself in another host, not the Eternal Darkness like he had thought he was heading. The host's body was smaller than the average adult. Apophis saw that he was laying in a bed with other beds around him with children. Apophis was slightly confused on why an adult would sleep in a room of children, Apophis got off the bed and went to the nearest mirror. What he saw was shocking to him. He was shocked to find himself in the body of a ten-year-old body.

For the purposes of the story, we will name this host Sam. Apophis heard voices of the adults in the facility shouting and screaming orders at other adults. Apophis looked around his surroundings, he saw that the factory he was in. Apophis saw that the sounds and designs of the structure was of some sort of specialized factory.

"Sam, I need you to go to sector 4 to get the bolts tightened on machine 4." A floor manager said walking into the room full of children.

"Yes sir, right away." Sam said heading towards the door of the room.

Apophis took control for just a moment before passing the manager.

"Excuse me sir, what year is it?" Apophis said.

"1840, now get to sector 4 quickly." The floor manager said not questioning why Sam would ask that.

"Yes sir, right away." Apophis said switching back with his host so he could figure out his new environment.

Apophis went to the memories and learned that Sam was an orphan, he lived and worked at the factory, the factory owner owned a great many orphan children. Each one was there to help get between machines, even taught to repair them. These children were paid 3 cents an hour plus food and a bed to sleep on. Each child worked 16-to-18-hour shifts.

The children both boys and girls shared a large room full of cots to sleep on, these children didn't talk much to each other because of the exhaustion from the work they were doing. Every once in a while, a child would be replaced with a new orphan child because the one that was in the cot before hand was killed by a machine. There were memories of burying the child in a grave in the back of the factory.

Sam felt lonely and depressed because he felt as if no one cared for him. All he knew was work and sleep. He had never known the love of a mother or father; he had no family or anyone to love him.

Apophis felt bad for the child, Apophis could relate on feeling alone because since the beginning of the banishment, he has felt alone. Apophis decided to help his host out and find him a companion or girlfriend to try and make him feel better.

Lights out was around 8:30pm, Sam and the other children each got in their individual cots. Sam fell asleep withing five minutes from the exhaustion of the busy day.

When Sam was fully asleep, Apophis took control of the body. Apophis got up and looked around until he spotted one of the orphan girls that was asleep in her own cot on the girl's side of the room. Apophis got up and went over to the young orphan girl's cot.

"Mandy, wake up." Apophis said tapping the girl on the shoulder to awaken her.

Mandy's eyes opened; her face showed surprise that Sam was near her bed.

"Sam, go back to your bed and got to sleep before you get us in trouble." Mandy said frightened of being disciplined.

"I will once I tell you that I like you, I always have, and we should hang out more and talk more. I know you feel a deeper connection to you, I hope you feel the same about me." Apophis said pretending to be Sam.

"Awe, Sam that is sweet, yes I do feel the same way about you. Now, please got back to your bed before we get in trouble." Mandy said kissing Apophis on the cheek.

Apophis kissed her on the cheek then turned to go back to his bed. On his way back to his bed, Apophis heard some adults roaming around. Curiosity got the better of Apophis, that he went to investigate what the adults were doing.

Apophis went up some stairs, when he got up to the top of the stairs, he saw a light on with two men in the room talking. Apophis used his excellent hearing to eavesdrop on the conversation.

"There are rumors of Mexican Terrorists destroying American weapons factories. I have this place and each child insured for if they were to die, I would get $85 a child that dies in an accident and as for the equipment is $100 per machine. I was thinking that we set fire to the factory with these children trapped inside. Then we should make a media spin that Mexican Terrorists attacked the factory thinking the factory was making weapons." The boss that owns and runs the factory said.

"Sir, are you sure that is wise?" The other gentleman said that was in the room.

"Yes, we are losing money in this factory, with it's destruction, we will make over $200,000 from the insurance claim." The boss said with a greedy tone in his voice.

Apophis was shocked how far could go for material money and wealth. But could he judge the humans so harshly? When the council is the same way, killing innocents for power and control.

The humans and the council were exactly the same in that sense, in fact the whole species is an exact image of how the council is. This journey has shown Apophis much, he has seen how evil and forgiving this world is, while he was powerless to do nothing at the moment.

After ten minutes of listening, Apophis saw the boss and the other gentleman step out of the office, and head to a large storage room full of gun powder and oils.

The boss made sure these were all piled next to each other as close as possible. The gentleman ripped up some rags and piled them in front of the gun powder and oil barrels.

Apophis watched them working on the destruction of the factory, he knew deep down he could not stop them, but he did know he could try to save the kids and his host. Apophis quietly turned and went back down to where the kids were sleeping. Apophis tried to awaken all the kids, but to no avail, they would not awaken due to taking such long hard shifts in the factory that all the orphan children were heavy sleeper. Apophis wasn't sure what to do.

Meanwhile, the boss and his associate were finishing off preparing for the destruction of the factory. The boss threw a match onto the pile of rags in front of the barrels of powder and oil. The boss and his associate evacuated the factory, when they got halfway up the stair, a loud explosion from down below shook the ground. The explosion could be heard throughout the factory.

Apophis saw as all the children awoken from the sound of the explosion. Every child was screaming and panicking. Every child was confused and crying not knowing what to do.

"Everyone! Listen to me! Calm down! We are going to get out of here together, just follow me." Apophis shouted to get everyone to listen.

The children all quieted down and looked towards Apophis. The Explosions continued. Apophis told the 3,000 children to follow him. None of the children listened they were too frighted to do anything. Apophis didn't know what to do. Mandy came up to Apophis and hugged him.

"Mandy, we all need to get out of here." Apophis said hugging her back.

"We are too later, all the exits are blocked and caved in, I just checked. The flames are getting closer." Mandy said giving up.

Apophis was confused and not sure how to get these kids out of here.

After 20 minutes, the flames had engulfed Apophis and the 3,000 children. One final explosion took out the entire factory, Apophis was sent back into the Eternal Darkness, his flesh was burning from the explosion.

Apophis floated there in the dark abyss, he stared into the darkness. Apophis felt a cold sense of dread running down his spine. Apophis saw that the darkness was further than he can see. Apophis felt a blanket of depression engulfed him; he didn't know how to stop it.

Unknown host #10

Apophis floated there in the Eternal Darkness, he felt his hatred grow for the Council. He thought to himself on how could he defeat such a powerful group? He was essentially powerless, he had no army, barely enough powers to even defeat the Council.

Within minutes of Apophis thinking to himself, a light engulfed him, Apophis was transferred into a new host. This host was in a military uniform, this was a blue uniform. For the purpose of the story, we are going to name this host Hartford.

Apophis looked around; he was at some sort of base that was made of stone. This base was a fort of some sort. Apophis walked out of the tiny room he was in. He stubbed into another officer.

"Private Hartford, drinking a little too much there?" the officer said.

"No, I just did see you there. I am sorry, what year is it and where are we?" Apophis asked.

"1845, San Antonio, Texas. Our mission is to keep this fort defended from Santa Anna's Mexican army." The officer said.

Apophis looked confused, he didn't know he was put in the middle of a war or the beginnings of one. Apophis walked down the hall and found a large room, that had a shrine for those that died in the *Texas Revolution*.

Apophis found a newspaper mentioning the issues between the United States, Texas, and Mexico. Apophis learned that Mexico didn't want to give up the Texas territory to the United States just because they United states was gaining territory as it expanded westward.

According to the paper, Texas wanted to be independent, Mexico wanted to control Texas as part of Mexico, The United States of America wanted to control Texas land as part of the United States. Apophis learned that his host as well as over 115,000 soldiers were sent to San Antonio to assist in any invasion of the Mexican army.

Apophis felt his host take back control and go to the nearest bar in the city. When Hartford got to a bar, one of the attendees, who was already plastered drunk recognized him.

"Hey, Hartford! Are you a yellow belly coward?" The attendee said challenging him.

"That is private, yellow belly coward to you, sir." Hartford said grabbing is pistol and aiming it at the guy.

Before he could let off the first shot, everyone else in the bar pulled out their pistols and shot him first. Apophis was tossed back into the Eternal Blackness.

Apophis was confused on why his last host was so weak, it was too quick to be killed.

"How are you handling your torment, Apophis?" A familiar voice said from behind Apophis.

Apophis turned around to see who the familiar voice was, a sheer shot of anger came forward. When Apophis saw it was RA standing there in front of him, he could not contain his rage. Apophis charged towards RA with full strength. RA froze Apophis in place about three inches from his face. Apophis tried to move and fight it, but it was unable to.

"Now, Now, Apophis, I was here to give to give you some personal assurance that your suffering will end sooner if you behave and follow the rules." RA said with a mischievous grin upon his face.

Apophis felt that RA was lying, he knew not to trust him. Apophis felt a sweat go down his face. RA walked around Apophis, studying him, he scoffed at Apophis. RA turned his back to Apophis then snapped his fingers unfreezing Apophis.

Apophis fell to the ground.

"Why should I trust you? You have lied before. You can rot in the sun and go away from here and leave me be." Apophis said holding back his rage.

RA grinned at Apophis and chuckled as he left without saying another word to Apophis. Apophis was alone in the Eternal Darkness. Apophis felt his rage and depression creep up on him. The Eternal Darkness brings depression and rage out. There is no stopping such emotions coming forth into the Eternal Darkness. In the Eternal Darkness, there is no time, light, feeling of hunger or thirst, love or peace. There are always sense of dread and depression in the Eternal Darkness.

Unknown host #11

Apophis placed his hands on his face with despair and frustration. While his hands were on his face, a flash of light transported him into a new host body. Apophis still had his hand on his face which translated over to the host.

For the purpose of this story, we will call this host Gregory.

"What happened, Gregory? Were you drinking again?" A soldier's voice said that was sitting right next to the bed Apophis was laying on.

Apophis removed his hands from his face and looked to his right side to see a soldier in blue uniform sitting in a chair.

Apophis looked around and saw that he was in a cloth tent of some sort. Apophis realized that he was in the middle of another war again. Apophis turned to look at the soldier.

"Yes, I think I bumped my head by accident that I forgot a few things." Apophis said.

The soldier looked at Apophis and chuckled a little to himself.

"Well, let me recover your memory for you, we are part of General Zachary Taylor's battalion. We are near Palo Alto valley to defend the United States against the Mexican army." The soldier said full of confidence.

Apophis was trying to process all what he was just told. The soldier got up from the chair to leave.

"Okay, before you go, one more thing I've got to ask you. What year is it?" Apophis asked.

The soldier turned facing Apophis and laughed a bit.

"That must have been some hit to the head to forget the year we are in. the year is 1846." The soldier mocked and laughed as he left the tent.

Apophis let go of control of the host body. He let his host Gregory back in control of the body. Apophis went to the back of the host's mind to think and observe. Apophis knew that he was centuries away from the end of his banishment. Apophis had only been a little over half a century of the banishment and he had learned so much about humans and their sicknesses and the exactness they are with the council. Apophis felt that even though he would try to escape into his own world the council would always be there, watching his every move. Bastet appeared to Apophis interrupted his thought process.

"Don't ruin this one, don't try to save him, let his destiny take its own course of action." Bastet said.

Apophis looked at Bastet with annoyance.

"Why? Am I always to feel the pain of the death?" Apophis asked with irritation in his voice.

"Yes, the Council will destroy you, if you help any host from now on. It is part of the punishment that you feel all pains of the deaths." Bastet said.

"Why must you keep reminding me about this?" Apophis frustratedly asked.

"The Council decrees that I must." Bastet said.

"Fuck the Council. Those rotten turds can suck my butt and feet. They are weak and this just proves that the don't want to fight a fair war." Apophis said with anger and arrogance in his voice.

Bastet remained silent for a moment, shaking her head in disappointment.

"If you are not going to provide me anything useful, then stop doing your check-ins on me!" Apophis said with rage in his voice.

Bastet stayed firm and quietly walked away fading into the blackness of the back of the mind.

The next morning, Apophis heard explosions outside of his host's tent. Apophis grabbed his host's gun and ran outside of the tent.

When he got outside, Apophis saw other soldiers running and scrambling to get to their defense positions. As the cannon fire continued, over a dozen or so soldiers were killed in the initial attack from the cannon fire.

Apophis was loading his weapon, when a Mexican battalion was storming the camp. Apophis had hidden behind some barrels of water. Apophis here cannon fire and bullets flying everywhere. Many soldiers on both sides were dying and having other casualties. Before Apophis could aim his weapon and fire it. He was shot and killed by a Mexican soldier.

About 15 seconds later, Apophis was back in the Eternal Darkness. Apophis had felt the coldness not from the ever darkness, but from his experience throughout the whole banishment.

Apophis learned from this experience is that humans are just as evil as those of the council that created them. Apophis could see the greed and pain that the Humans and Council both love so much.

Bastet appeared out of nowhere.

"What do you want?" Apophis snapped at Bastet.

"I wanted to ensure you that you that you are not losing your sanity." Bastet said.

"My sanity? Why would that be a concern to you?" Apophis scoffed at what Bastet just said to him.

Apophis found the whole fake concern for his sanity a bit ridiculous.

"I am just trying to be a friend to you in your trying times." Bastet said trying to show Apophis compassion and concern.

"A friend?" Apophis scoffed at that.

"Yes, I want you to trust me." Bastet said.

"Trust you? You and the Council voted for me to be in this banishment." Apophis snapped at Bastet.

Bastet stayed silent with a look of regret and guilt on her face.

"Maybe in time, you will come to forgive me for that and be my friend." Bastet said as she disappeared onto the darkness.

Unknown host #12

Shortly after Bastet had departed, Apophis was transported into a new host. This time he was in some sort of structure of peculiar design, but he had a strange feeling he had been there before. This fortification was alien but familiar at the same time. Apophis had entered this host in the plaza of this fort. Apophis turned his head to the left. There on the wall was a plaque that was about four feet long made of iron. Apophis walked up to it and saw that the place said, "In honor of those that had fallen in battle protecting this fort Alamo."

Apophis has a cold chill run down his spine as the realization sank in. Apophis had been in this fort before, but it looked different this time. Or was it his memory going out on him?

Apophis took another look around him; he knew it wasn't his memory, this place has changed since he was last in it. There was more damage than before.

Apophis was shocked that he didn't hear of the battle last time he was in a host. Apophis looked at the clothing that his host was wearing. He was surprised to find that his host was in the military.

For the purpose of this story, we will call this host Shoemaker.

"Shoemaker, it is time for you to rest, that is way too much alcohol." One of the other soldiers said to Apophis.

Apophis could tell that his host already drank 12 bottles of beer, Apophis felt a bit drunk. Apophis felt like vomiting, Apophis stumbled and fell over. A bunch of soldiers went over to Apophis, before he passed out, some medical soldiers took him to the medical tent.

After three hours of being unconscious, Apophis had awoken up, a nurse was attending to him.

"Ah, you are awake. Do you know where you are?" the nurse asked.

"No, where am I? What year is it?" Apophis asked.

"You are in the fort Alamo, in San Antonio, Texas. The year is 1848." The nurse said.

Apophis realized he was back in San Antonio, Texas once again. Apophis was shocked at all of this. Apophis let his host take back control.

Shoemaker was a bit dazed, he got up and told the nurse he was fine. The nurse let him leave. Shoemaker went to the local bar to get more to drink.

When shoemaker had entered the bar, he stumbled up to the bartender.

"I would like 12 large beers please sir." Shoemaker said plopping down two silver $5 coins. He also pulled out three gold eagle dollars all three being $10 pieces.

"Also, another 12 after that." Shoemaker said.

"Alright, but that is the last of my supply until December." The bar tender said putting the money away and giving shoemaker his drinks.

Shoemaker took his beers and was drinking as he was walking back to his quarters on base. As he opened the bottles and drank, one of the bottles had more alcohol than beer, but Shoemakers couldn't tell because he was too drunk.

Apophis felt his hosts body slowly dying from all the alcohol. Apophis could not stop his host from poisoning himself from all the alcohol. There was already over 30 in his system, and he kept drinking.

Before Shoemaker could make it to his quarters, he collapsed into a seizure fit, No one was around to help him. Moments later, Apophis was back in the Eternal Darkness.

Apophis didn't understand why that was drinking so much. He had so little time with him. Apophis wandered why it was such a short time.

As Apophis was thinking about why that host was so short lived, Anubis came forth out of the dark.

"Apophis you sly serpent, how goes your banishment?" Anubis said twitching his jackal ears.

"Its is hell, much like sniffing a different dog's ass each time." Apophis said chuckling a little knowing that offended Anubis.

Anubis growled and grabbed Apophis by the neck.

"You have not learned anything from your banishment, have you?" Anubis said tightening his grip around Apophis's throat.

"Shall I tell the council to extend the banishment until the end of time for that insult?" Anubis said releasing his grip on Apophis's throat.

Apophis dropped down, coughing trying to catch his breath.

"You wouldn't dare, you coward. Because you know that I can still strike fear into you even though, I'm banished." Apophis said still trying to catch his breath.

Anubis knew that it was true, the entire council were all afraid of Apophis deep down, but they dare not admit it. The council feared what Apophis could do to them, if Apophis ever found a way to regain power.

"You are too weak to destroy the entire Council, we would wipe you out in a blink of an eye." Anubis lied feeling a cold chill go down his spine, he became very uneasy.

Apophis grinned, knowing that he could destroy the Council in other ways as well, he would have to discover it first. Apophis could sense that he was make Anubis feel uneasy. Apophis also knew he could destroy the Council if he regained his power first, but he would be patient and wait to see which came first.

Anubis quickly left like a puppy with his tail between his legs.

Unknown host #13

Apophis was engulfed by the bright light again, once he had awoken in a large tent with fur pellets on the ground for bedding, in the confusion Apophis ran out of the tent. When Apophis made his way out of the tent, he saw Native American Indians, which in fact was something his former hosts wanted to oppress and control, except for the African slave he was in. For the purpose of this host, we will call him Crying wolf.

"Crying wolf, are you well?" A tribesman asked with concern in his voice.

Apophis was still a bit of lagged a bit sort of like a jetlag, he was a bit confused.

"Yes, just a night fear." Apophis said.

"Keep your spirits high, we will have our minds clear soon." The tribesman said.

Apophis was confused on what that was supposed to mean. After the tribesman walked away, Apophis went about the tribal camp. Apophis found the whole camp, so alien and primitive compared to the architecture of ancient Egypt that he was used to. Apophis thought back to his time, where he had a palace and servants to wait on him hand and foot. Apophis never knew he was going to have a host that lived in a tent. Apophis felt his host take back control. Apophis went to the back of his host's mind and just observed his host sneaking into another tribe's camp, with a heavy log. He crept behind three of the most beautiful of the women of the tribe. Each one was distracted with a task of making clothes.

Crying wolf raised the log above his head and hit each of the women on the back of the head. Once they were knocked unconscious, Crying wolf quickly and swiftly dragged them out of the tent. Crying wolf place each of the women on his horse with arms and feet bound, as well as their mouths gagged.

Apophis was shocked that his host did that, and the fact that the rest of the tribe wasn't alerted to the sound of the women being hit over the head.

Apophis saw his host go to an abandoned cabin, that was abandoned by settlers 12 years earlier. Crying wolf dragged each woman off his horse and into the abandon cabin one by one. Apophis saw his host's thoughts, He learned that his host was to meet some white men from the local town, seven miles away from the abandoned cabin. Crying wolf tied each of the three women to three separate beds in the cabin.

When Crying wolf finished tying up each woman, he pulled a knife out from his sheath on his waist. Crying wolf went to each woman and began to cut their clothes off. Once finished, he had all three women completely naked, he admired all three women's beautiful bodies and breasts. He went to each woman and touched their bodies and raped each one after the other. Apophis was disgusted at seeing his host raping a woman. Apophis would never had done that to a woman that didn't want him or anyone else. Apophis believes in consensual sex and love. Crying wolf took 45 minutes to rape each woman, Crying wolf was trying the "product out" before selling it to the customer so to speak. Apophis was horrified as the sight he was seeing, he wished he could stop this, but he knew the council would surely stop him from interfering.

3 hour later, Crying wolf was cleaning each woman up and ensuring that they looked presentable, but he left the naked for the men that he was going to sell these women to, would want to see the nude bodies.

A knock at the door came, Crying wolf stood up and went to the door to answer it. When he opened the door, there were two 6-foot-tall white men, both wearing black jackets, black chaps, black hats, black shirt, black pants and black boots.

"Red skin boy, where are the women that we are here to buy from you." One of the white men said.

"Right, do you have payment first before I allow you in?" Crying wolf said with greed in his voice.

The second white man pulled out a large box that was well hidden between the two, he opened it exposing gold coins. Apophis was amazed at how much gold coins that was in the box for three women. Apophis quickly hatched a plan to hide that gold for himself, he would just need the right moment to take control. Crying wolf's eye grew large like two large pieces of coal.

Crying wolf took the box and then lead the two men into the cabin. The two men saw the women and went over to each one examining them. The two men touched each woman across her body from her face to her breasts to her vagina and anus.

"These women are perfect, we will need you to find double as many women next week and we will pay, double next time." One of the white men said extending out his hand to close a deal.

"We have ourselves a deal." Crying Wolf said excited.

The two men and crying wolf carried the women out the white men's covered wagon. When the two men departed, Crying Wolf laid down on the bed and started to feel a bit sick. He decided to sleep. Before Apophis could take control of the body, he was suddenly back in the Eternal Darkness, this time without feeling any pain. Apophis was confused on what had just happen.

Bastet walked into the Eternal Darkness.

"Why am I back in the Eternal Darkness, so soon?" Apophis asked.

Bastet stared at Apophis for a moment.

"Your last host had Syphilis, which got to his brain and killed him in his sleep." Baset said.

Apophis looked at Bastet with suspicion that it was more of a reason than what Bastet was letting on.

"It is strange on how I laid eyes on the gold, that I could have hidden that from my host for myself, then to suddenly die the night I discovered it, seems odd to me. Doesn't it to you?" Apophis said with suspicion and rage in his voice.

Bastet kept quiet, she was getting nervous, her hairs on the back of her neck were being to stand up.

"Did the Council have something to do with that?" Apophis demanded.

Bastet hesitated for a moment, until she cracked from the pressure.

"Yes, they did. They don't want you to be able to hide any gold or other precious resources that you could use to gain power once again." Bastet said nervously.

Apophis's face turned blood red in anger.

"Why do they care so much? They banished me because they found me "guilty" for a crime I didn't commit!" Apophis screamed in rage.

Bastet quickly disappeared out of fear.

Apophis was raging alone in the Eternal Darkness; he was planning his revenge against the Council. He hopes one day to destroy the Council soon enough.

Unknown host #14

While he was feeling anger towards the Council, he was thrown into a new host. Apophis woke up in a very large bedroom that was large enough to put a sarcophagus and the treasures of the deceased in this room. Apophis was amazed at how large the room was compared to his previous hosts.

Apophis got up off the bed, which was made of the most comfortable material of the time and handcrafted footboard and headboard. The wood of the headboard and footboard was crafted by hand from cherry wood. Apophis had not seen such beauty before. Apophis ran his hand along the headboard and footboard. Apophis noticed that the dresser was made of the same wood and as well as the vanity desk, even the two nightstands that were in the room.

Apophis turned to examine the room he was in, everything in the room was of the best quality. Apophis saw two large double doors; I believe you would call them "French doors". Apophis walked over to the doors and opened them to discover another large room with a bath, mirrors and assorted makeups from the best designers of the time.

Apophis was confused on what all the makeups were for. Apophis, in his time, wore only a limited amount of makeup to ensure he was known for his rule and to keep lice away. Back in Ancient Egypt, where makeup was invented essentially, makeup was worn by both men and women because they were using them for the lice and other ecological issues besides status and attraction. Egyptian makeup was more essential, then that of today.

Yes, Makeup back then was mostly used to keep the mites out of the eyes and helped regulate body temperature, in Egypt the temperature would get hot, fashion and makeup is what your society owes a debt of gratitude to ancient Egypt. -Apophis

Apophis found all this strange to him, it was so foreign to him, in all his years of life and banishment. Apophis felt nervous, these things are so alien.

The door in the next room opened, a maid walked into the room. Apophis walked back into the room; the maid looked shocked.

For the purpose of this host, we will name this host Amanda.

"I am sorry, miss Amanda. I didn't know you were in the nude." The maid said.

Apophis looked down and saw a young white girl's body with perfectly curved legs, hips that scream perfection. This body could have belonged to a goddess. There were perfectly small breasts about a 34b, blonde hair, this host was in her early 20's, about 21 or 22 years of age.

"Servant girl, what year is it? Also where are we located?" Apophis asked sounding a bit demanding.

The maid looked confused for a moment, then answered the question.

"The year is 1854, we are in your father's plantation in Mississippi." The maid answered.

Apophis took a moment to process the fact he is nearly a century into the banishment. Apophis feels that he has only been in the banishment for five years. The only reason he feels like that is because of the time dilation feeling he is experiencing every time a host dies and he ends up in the Eternal Darkness.

"Thank you, I am hungry, what is there to eat?" Apophis asked.

"There are fresh grapes with croissants and fresh jam, as well as sausages and hot cakes with fresh butter." The maid said.

Apophis thought for a moment, it had been a long while since he had such wonderful choices.

"I will take both with extra sausages about six extra to be exact, please." Apophis ordered.

The maid's eyes got huge like a deer in the head lights of a car at the request.

"Miss, you are watching your figure, your mom says you must watch what you eat." The maid protests.

Apophis was surprised at how the maid was back talking at a request of a superior.

"Are you back talking me? You are the help, follow orders or else." Apophis threatened.

"Sorry, Miss I'll get your food right away." The maid said turning to leave the room.

As soon as the maid left the room, Apophis rejoiced at the host he was placed into. He knew with the privileges that this host has. Apophis planned to try and hide some of the wealth away for him to use in another host down the road.

Suddenly, Apophis felt that the host would die sooner than he thought. A flash of a future memory, a premonition of sorts. The premonition was of a ball that was in two days. Apophis felt the host's stress, anxiety, and depression, he felt the host wanted a gentleman from England to dance with her.

Just as the food arrived, the vision ended. Apophis saw the tray of delicious food; he began to salivate. Once the maid set the tray of food down on the vanity desk.

Apophis began to devour the food like a wild animal. The maid's mouth dropped in shock as she saw Apophis devour the food like there was no tomorrow. The maid had never seen the host not use her manners that were ingrained into here since the beginning.

Apophis was halfway into his meal when he was ripped out of control of the host body into the back of the mind. Apophis was stunned and confused, until Bastet walked into the blackness of the back of the host's mind.

When Apophis was switched with the host, the host, Amanda was in a daze like state, she was confused, until she saw the tray of food. She stared at the food and began to complain.

"Why is there so much food here? I only eat bread and grapes, take this food away." Amanda demanded.

The maid looked confused on what just happened.

"Miss Amanda, are you feeling well? You requested me to get this food, a little while ago." The maid said.

"I am bloody fine, now. Leave me alone." Amanda snapped at the maid.

The maid took the tray of food and left the room, still confused on what was going on. She felt that the master's daughter was cracking up and losing her mind, but she could not say anything because she could lose her job.

Meanwhile, deep in the mind, Apophis was staring at Bastet angrily. He knew he lost his meal now that Bastet has intervened.

"I was enjoying my meal, Bitch!" Apophis hissed.

"Apophis, you cannot take advantage of the wealth and privilege of the host. You need not to intervene, you are there to learn your lesson." Bastet scolded whipping her tail.

Apophis glared at Bastet, knowing that she and the Council were arrogant. Bastet turned to leave Apophis in the back of the mind.

The moment Bastet turned and disappeared; Apophis took went to watch the host and how she interacts with her environment.

"Servant! Where are my silver rings? I need them shined for the party tonight, hurry!" Amanda was barking orders at the servants.

Apophis watched as this was going on, Apophis felt a deep disappointment on how he was placed in such a spoiled rotten child. In Apophis's time, he would have disciplined such a rude child, Apophis wandered who this host's parents were.

While Apophis was watching the chaos happening, the girl's mother walked in the room.

"Amanda! Why are you not bathed for the party tonight?" The mother asked.

"Mother, I've been stressing over everything, bathing slipped my mind." Amanda said.

Amanda's mother was a thin white woman, with blonde hair, icy blue eyes. She wore the most expensive silk dresses of the time, which was worth its weight in gold. Her mother was the same height as Amanda, they both were about five foot four inches tall, she was in her late thirties. Apophis was shocked to see such clothes with that material. In his time, there was either animal skins or cotton material for clothing.

"Hurry Amanda, we have hours until the guests arrive for the party. Also, stick to salads and water, that way you can keep thin. No meats or bread, ladies only nibble and have small meals." The mother said.

Apophis felt enraged from what he was hearing that he took control of the host's body.

"Mother, speak for yourself your ass is the size of the moon." Apophis said pissed off on the diet restrictions the mother has imposed on her daughter.

Amanda's Mother slapped her across the face, that felt like a hard paddle to the face, while Apophis was in control, long before he could switch back with Amanda, Apophis felt the full blow of the slap that he was even more enraged.

"HOW DARE YOU INSULT ME LIKE THAT!!!" The mother screamed raising her hand for another blow to the face.

Apophis was beyond enraged at this point, just before the hand could hit his face again, Apophis grabbed the mother's arm midair, stopping her from slapping again. Apophis glared at the mother.

"Look Mother, you really get yourself on a nice long walk or run for that matter, you need to lose your big fat ass." Apophis festered the problem more causing more issues with the mother.

Apophis saw the mother's face turn as red as a hot stone that is steaming. Veins were popping out of her face. Apophis grinned and then switch control with Amanda.

Amanda was still holding her mother's arm midair; she was confused on what was going on. Amanda quickly let go of her mother's arms and then came a huge slap across the face that was so hard that Amanda was on the ground in pain.

"HOW RUDE YOU HAVE BEEN TO ME! YOU HAVE LOST THREE MONTHS ALLOWANCE FOR INSULTING ME LIKE THAT!" The mother screamed at Amanda.

Amanda had tears in her eyes, she turned to look at her mother with tears running down her face. She was confused on what she was talking about insulting her.

"You are evil. I hate you. I didn't even say any insults to you. I blacked out, we were talking about food last, I remember." Amanda said with tears running down her face.

"You are lying, you call my ass as big as a moon." The mother said thrusting her leg to kick Amanda who was still on the ground.

Amanda felt the painful blow of the kick and she passed out from the pain.

Apophis laughed at the humor he saw with both these spoiled women, a mother that is spoiled by status and a daughter that is spoiled by privilege and status as well.

Moments later, Amanda awoke, she quickly got up and began to rush through her closet to get a dress for tonight's party. Apophis could feel that Amanda was under a lot of social pressure, which in turn gave her extreme anxiety, especially when thoughts of this party ran through her mind.

Apophis saw that Amanda, his host had a crush on a prince from Germany, she found this young prince very attractive. She wanted to be his queen, she imagined herself sitting next to him in her own throne that is next to his throne.

Amanda ran a warm water bath, she put lavender soap in the water that was homemade. Amanda began to strip down naked. She put one foot in the water, then the other, she laid down in the water completely covered in the warm water. The body was tingling from the warmth of the water. Amanda grabbed a bar of soap and began to wash her body starting at her chest. She washed her breasts, belly, arms, legs, then hips. Apophis didn't want to watch his host bathe, so he went to the memories to try and learn more about this party.

Apophis saw that this party invites people from across the world from a dozen countries. The rich and elite were all to be there. The whole thing is amazing, these parties happen three times a year. This specific party was a Halloween party. Apophis felt a cold chill run down his spine. He knew his children would hunt him down here. They were still enraged with him; Apophis didn't know how to avoid them. His children can take any shape they choose. He would only know that they are there by the essence sense, like a sixth sense type. Much like your intuition, but much stronger.

After 40 minutes, Amanda got out of the bath, drained it and began to dry off and get dressed. In the next room, the servant walked in with a message.

"Ma'am, your mother sent me to help you with your makeup, the party is in one hour." The servant said.

"Yes, thank you, come into the powder room." Amanda said politely and calmly.

After an hour of getting Amanda's makeup and hair done. Amanda left the room and went to the stairs case; she began her descent down the stairs. Once she got to the bottom of stairs, Apophis saw beautifully placed decorations and over one hundred and fifty guests at this party. This party was quite a grand party indeed.

Amanda walked around the grand ball room, smiling nervously and greeting everyone, she had crossed paths with.

Apophis saw through her eyes that there were ambassadors from over two dozen countries. When Amanda came near the table of food and the most expensive wine, Apophis's jaw dropped at the sheer sight of it. The food was enough to feed a large army or 12 Gods and Goddesses. Apophis took over control of the body.

Apophis went straight to the table of food; he grabbed a plate. His eyes got huge like a fat kid's eyes in a candy shop at all the food that laid out before him. Apophis saw roast beef, roasted ham, rib racks of both beef and pork, steaks piled high on platters, deer meats, fruits from all across the world, exotic rice, and wines as well other drinks from across the world. Apophis began to grab all the meats he could grab and place on the plate. He even poured himself some wine. Apophis was curious about the exotic fruits especially a stinky fruit that was sitting on the table, Apophis grabbed a small piece of the stinky fruit.

About two minutes after trying the fruit, Apophis vomited all over the floor. Apophis realized that the fruit was not good for ingesting.

"AMANDA! That is unlady like, you need to go to your room and change!" Amanda's mother screamed in embarrassment.

Apophis took his plate of food with him to the bedroom. He was feasting while walking to the room the spectators that watched him eat were all gasping and shocked that he could eat after vomiting a lot.

After 20 minutes, Amanda was back in control and was confused on why she was in a different dress. She went back down to the ball room, looking for her mother, until she ran into the prince of Germany. Amanda Turned deep red in embarrassment and shyness.

"Hello, Sir Fredrick." Amanda said.

"Hello, fraulein Amanda, have you seen my wife?" Fredrick said.

"Your wife?" Amanda said with shock and disappointment in her voice, her heart sank deep. Fredrick didn't notice the tone of her voice.

"Yes, I seemed to have lost her at the grand banquet." Fredrick said.

"I haven't seen her, I forgot something in my room, I must wish you good night and I shall return to the party later." Amanda said retreating back to her room closing and locking the door.

Amanda burst into tears, every thought in Amanda's head was that her life was over and that there was no point in going on anymore. Amanda decided to end her life. Amanda went over to the bathtub and ran the water, as the water was running, Amanda went over to the closet and pulled out a wooden box and pulled out a 12-inch bladed knife.

Amanda disrobed and stepped in the water with the blade in hand. Amanda shut off the water, held the blade two inches from her heart and with one swift motion of her wrist she stabbed herself in the heart, Apophis felt the blade pierce into Amanda's heart for a few seconds before he was sent back into the Eternal Darkness.

Apophis was alone in the Eternal Darkness, waiting for his next host. While Apophis was awaiting to go into go into his next torturous experience in a host, Bastet arrived into the blackness.

"You know the rules, you were not supposed to intervene, not even for a meal." Bastet scolded.

"What? I was supposed to let the perfect meal pass me by?" Apophis said.

"Yes, and you could have avoided running into that prince." Bastet said.

"You are blaming me for the suicide? That is rich coming from you, you pawn of the council." Apophis scoffed.

"Well, you caused a fight between mother and daughter." Bastet said.

"That is not entirely true, that mother was already having her daughter fight her before I showed up. Quit lying and making me look like the bad guy." Apophis said.

Bastet knew that he was right, she couldn't guilt trip him for anything. Bastet's skin tightened with rage.

"You will never learn your lesson, you slithering slug." Bastet insulted.

"Lesson? There are no lessons in the cruel banishment, even I was to 'learn' a lesson. Do you really think the Council will let me be free in my true form?" Apophis sneered back.

Bastet stayed silent, knowing deep down that the truth was that there was no way the Council will ever let Apophis free. She knew that he would be going from host to host until the end of the universe and the start of the next universe.

Unknown host #15

Bastet turned and left Apophis alone floating there alone in the darkness. Within moments after she had departed Apophis was transported to another host.

For the purpose of this story, we will name this host Alexander.

Apophis saw that he was in a room full of strange things that he had never seen before. There was a table with a silver cloth on top of it. On top of the cloth was a crystal ball in the middle of the table. On the walls were poster the said "Alexander the great, psychic readings"

Apophis let out a large laugh at how pathetically hilarious the sign was.

Apophis knew that psychic powers were real, but he knew only select people were actually aware of them. He sensed that this host was a scammer. Apophis walked over to the table and saw on the table was a newspaper. Apophis picked up the paper and looked at the year on the paper. It was 1857, suddenly there was a ding at the door. Apophis went to open the door.

Apophis opened the door, there stood a young woman, about the age of his last host, she walked through the door, the young woman in her almond-colored complexion shined through her scarf, her cheek bones were smooth as polished alabaster stone.

"Sir, I need your help, I need to know my fortune regarding a job I found here. I want to know if it is a guaranteed job for me." The young woman said.

Apophis was shocked and curious about this young woman, before he could ask her other details about her, Bastet had pulled Apophis into the back of the host's mind.

"What the hell do you want now, Feline?" Apophis demanded.

"I pulled you out of control to tell you that, you are not supposed to have any love interests, the council will punish you greatly for that, if you do. Also, teach tis host a lesson, he has been a nuisance to this whole world, even in the next world as well. He has scammed many people, he even has caught the attention of Anubis. Anubis wants him dead." Bastet said.

"Wait, what has this host done to get the attention of Anubis?" Apophis said curiously.

"Well, this host you are in had cancer six months ago, he contacted Anubis to make a deal for his soul to let him heal from cancer, but it turned out to be a scam, the cancer really was not going to kill him in three days is what he had told Anubis." Bastet said.

"So, dog boy and you want me to do your dirty work and kill someone that has burned you?" Apophis said.

"Yes, it is the best way." Bastet said.

"What does the Council say about this?" Apophis said.

"They agree that you must do it." Bastet said.

Apophis paused for a moment. He thought deeply, he knew if he agreed to this, the council would use it against him.

"No, I will not do it." Apophis declared.

Bastet's tail twitched in annoyance.

"Suit yourself, see how quickly he will be a nuisance to you." Bastet warned as she turned to leave into the darkness in the back of the mind.

Apophis was alone in the back of the host mind; he went to watch what Alexander was doing to help the young woman that Apophis had taken a liking to.

Alexander was sitting in front of the crystal ball on the table, and the young woman was sitting in front of him. Alexander was staring into the crystal ball not truly focusing or seeing anything.

"I see that you will be the head manager in six months' time, and you will move into a beautiful two-story home that overlooks a valley." Alexander lied convincingly to the young woman.

"Sir, will I be rich?" the young woman asked handing Alexander $300 dollars from her purse.

"MMM… I call upon the great spirits, show me this woman's answer to her question!" Alexander commanded.

The candles flickered as they were set to do, by a small breeze that came in from a crack in the wall. Apophis laughed at the sight of the scammer faking looking into the crystal ball, so Apophis gave Alexander a true vision. Apophis showed him the truth of his scam, the lady in the vision was dirt poor, begging for food and money on the streets.

Alexander gasped.

"What is it, sir? What did you see?" The young woman said curiously.

Alexander focused back to his track of scamming and lying.

"I saw that you will have great riches to where you can quit your job, also you will also own 12 homes. You will walk the high life." Alexander lied again to the young woman, knowing he saw the truth.

The young woman's face gleamed with excitement in her face. She could hardly contain her joy from the news. She got up to leave, as she was leaving, she paid Alexander another $500 dollars and thanked him for his prophecy he had given her.

"Come again, my dear." Alexander said closing the door.

Apophis got annoyed on how low this host was to that poor girl. Apophis had to come up with a plan to help Anubis to get this guy's soul for his Judgement. Apophis couldn't believe that Bastet was right, this guy needed to be killed even though that meant Apophis was going back into the Eternal Darkness.

Alexander went over to the calendar that was hanging on the wall, He noticed that tomorrow was Halloween, his busiest day of the year to get clients.

"Perfect, I should go to the store to get some candy and other treats." Alexander thought to himself as he prepared to go to the store.

Apophis knew Tomorrow, Halloween should be the day Anubis will get this guy's soul.

As Alexander was stepping out the door, A large gentleman in his mid-30's, muscular, in a suit, stood on the front stoop(**For those not in the know, the word stoop means a porch with steps in the front of a house or building).**

"Yes, I hear you are the man to talk about futures and fortunes." The gentleman said in a smug sarcastic voice.

"That I am, sir. Come sit down and I will read your future and fortune." Alexander said leading the gentleman to the table.

The gentleman sat down on the opposite side of the table, as Alexander sat down.

"How would you like your future read? Tarot? Crystal Ball? Palm? I specialize in all three types." Alexander said.

The gentleman paused for a moment; he had a look of regret on his face for his choice.

"Well, how about Crystal Ball." The gentleman laughed under his breath.

Apophis saw an opportunity to give this guy a worse false prophecy than what Alexander had planned. Apophis took over Alexander's body.

"Let's begin." Apophis said staring into the crystal ball and waving his hands over the ball.

After ten minutes of Apophis waving his arms over the crystal ball. Apophis "Pretended" to see a vision.

"Ah, yes. I see you will inherit a country in six hours, you are to be king of an island nation. You didn't know you were royalty, did you?" Apophis said.

The gentleman's face went from regretful expression to a shocked look.

"Thank you, Alexander." The gentleman said, pulling $2,000 dollars out of a bag he was carrying.

After paying, the gentleman swiftly left the shop. Apophis knew he had six more hours in this host's body, before the gentleman would realize the prophecy was a lie. Apophis knew that this host would be killed by that gentleman.

Alexander was in the back of his mind, asleep for all he knew, was that he was drunk with no memory of the gentleman arriving. Apophis took the $2,000 dollars to the store. He was going to get himself some food, he doesn't know when he would be able to eat again.

When Apophis arrived at the local grocery store, he saw meats, chocolates from the *Whitman Company*. Apophis bought $1,000 dollars of meat and a $1,000 dollars' worth of chocolate, if he was going back into the Eternal darkness, he wanted to enjoy his last few hours.

After making his way back to the shop, Apophis cooked the meat he had bought while dining on Chocolate. The taste of the chocolate was delicious. Apophis had never tasted anything so savory and sweet. This was the first time he had ever tried chocolate. The previous hosts never had chocolate, The chocolate was either unavailable to the host or he was in the host for too short of a time to try it.

After about three hours of Apophis enjoying his meat and chocolate, a knock came at the front door, loud enough to wake the dead.

Apophis went to open the door, when he opened the door, the door was swung open from the other side by a massive force, the sheer force knocked Apophis to the ground. The gentleman from earlier walked into the opened door, he was angered. He began to yell at Apophis.

"YOU LIED TO ME; I AM NOT ROYALTY! I WANT MY $2000 DOLLARS BACK!" The gentlemen screamed at the top of his lungs, Apophis's ears felt as if they were about to burst from the sheer volume of the gentleman's voice.

"I don't have the money, I spent it. May I offer you some steak and chocolate." Apophis said getting up, grabbing the chocolate and offering it to the Gentleman.

The gentleman smacked the chocolate out of Apophis's hands, Apophis watch the chocolate in slow motion as it fell to the ground. He heart sank at the sight of such a waste of great chocolate.

The gentleman quickly pulled out a knife from his belt that was a Bowie knife, and stabbed Apophis multiple times as he stared at the fallen chocolate on the ground. Before Apophis realized he was back in the Eternal darkness within minutes, all he could think of was the wasted chocolate on the ground.

Bastet appeared in the Eternal Darkness, walking up to Apophis. She noticed the sad look on Apophis's face.

"You did well, Anubis that host's soul and he has died a second death." Bastet said.

"Alright, do I get a reward for helping you guys apprehend that soul that you guys conveniently placed me in? you guys essentially owe me chocolates." Apophis said knowing the true answer was "no."

"No, there is no reward for helping us, it is your solemn duty to help us with unwanted souls, when you are placed in the as hosts." Bastet snapped at Apophis for asking such a ridiculous question.

"Is this whole banishment making you dumb?" Bastet taunted Apophis.

Apophis felt anger build up from what Bastet just said, he chose not to say anything to keep further punishment.

Bastet turned her back and left Apophis alone in the blackness once more.

Unknown host #16

Apophis sat there floating in the pitch blackness as black as an obsidian stone. Apophis was wandering I his thoughts, wandering when is his banishment ever going to end?

Within a matter of moments, a flash of light appeared, and Apophis was transported into another host body.

Apophis was in a chamber filled with other people debating on country issues, one specific issue that Apophis was listening to the issue of slavery, this surprised Apophis that the issue of slavery has become a social issue that these people in this chamber were debating on. Apophis was very bewildered, since slavery had been around as far back to his time or even paleolithic era as well. Mankind had always enslaved others of their kinds, either as captured enemies or purchased slaves. Of course, there has been cases of people volunteering themselves as slaves to pay off a debt to a creditor. When did all this change? Apophis, of course had slaves when he was in Egypt, but he was fair with his slaves, how did slavery become a moral issue?

"I know, Mr. President of congress that slavery has helped build America into what it is today, but those humans have a human right to a real life, a family, income, pay taxes, own property, with this our economy will boom more if slavery is abolished." A senator with silver white hair said.

For the purpose of this story, we will name this host Andrew.

"Slavery has helped our country; these slaves have contributed to our economy by receiving free housing and food. Their masters pay taxes on them, we should tax the masters a higher rate, and not free the slaves. If we do, our economy will fall." Southern congressman Andrew, Apophis's host said.

Apophis was shocked on the debates he was hearing, he had never heard such a ridiculous debating, not even the Egyptian Pharoah's would have sounded so weak, if they did, they people would have them killed.

"Look, Congressman Andrew, the world is evolving to make slavery obsolete, Manufacturing jobs are replacing slavery, and, in this year of 1860, it be said, I, Alex do not support slavery." The silver haired congressman said.

Apophis was shocked that he was nearing is first full century in his banishment, 1860 is only twenty-four years before the century, well anniversary, of his banishment, even though calling it an anniversary is a long stretch at best. Apophis didn't want to think of that, he doesn't like the constant reminder that he has been banished for so long.

"We shall end today's session; we shall resume tomorrow." The President of congress said slamming down his hammer.

Apophis's host stood and left the chamber and went to the outside Congressional Chamber house, he took a carriage to the local brothel house, upon his arrival, he stepped out of the carriage, he saw a young twenty-four-year-old, African American woman, he followed her down the street two block, knowing that no one at the time would believe a young African American girl that a white congressman raped her. Apophis saw the evil desire that his host had but couldn't take control because the host's urge was too strong.

He followed her until they got to a bit of an abandoned section the street, He grabbed her by her hair forcing her to the ground, he dragged her down a dark alley by her hair. When he got to a spot he was satisfied with, he preceded to undo her dress adding a few rips in it, the young girl tried to struggle, but he struck her a few times in the face with a balled fist. She was knocked unconscious for a moment; Andrew undid his pants and ripped the young girl's undergarments off. He positioned her for him to penetrate her vagina. He ramped in his penis, this briefly woke the young woman up, she struggled to get him off of her, she let out a scream from the pain, but Andrew covered her mouth with his hand as he began thrusting until he ejaculated inside her, once he finished, He removed his shoe and beat her over her head with his shoe, until she was dead.

Apophis was appalled from what he had just witnessed. Apophis had seen so many atrocities that his hosts have committed in his time of the banishment, but he could not blame his hosts for those atrocities, they inherited them from the Council. The Council has breed that into the human condition, it was part of their game.

Andrew pulled up his pants and fixed himself up, he walked out of the alley. He then walked to the nearest bar to get an alcoholic drink. The body of the young woman was left there in the alley to rotten, he knew no one could trace it back to him.

Apophis wandered why the council would place Apophis in such sadistic hosts, there has been too many that he has been in already. Bastet appeared behind Apophis.

"Enjoying the show?" Bastet sarcastically asked.

"This host is a bad person much like the shoemaker, Native American, and the scammer. Why are you guys sending me to hosts like this?" Apophis inquired.

"Because we can, you need not ask, Apophis, your punishment is to suffer all aspects of human lives. Be it you bare witness to the atrocities humans commit or not." Bastet said with a hiss of irritation in her voice.

Apophis could not believe what he was just told.

After saying what she said to Apophis, Bastet turned and disappeared out of view.

After Andrew finished with the bar, he called a carriage to get back home, on his way home, he vomited in the carriage. By the time he got home, he paid the drive, and stumbled to the house.

When Andrew got inside, there was an African American woman standing at attention like a military, her four young children were standing the same way, which is unusual for the ages of the children which were three years old, four years old, five years old, and six years old.

Andrew walked towards them like a harsh slave master, he got up close and personal in the woman's face. Her face was neutral, not breaking a sweat from nervousness, Andrew kissed her passionately, everyone broke character and were running up to him, laughing and hugging him.

Apophis was shocked that such a brutal person and murderous, being the family type.

"Father, can we have a pony?" The three-year-old child asked.

"Soon, maybe for Christmas." Andrew said.

Andrew, the African American maid and their four children all loved each other, but if anyone in this society of the time were to learn this, Andrew's reputation would be ruined, especially his position on Slavery.

"How were the deliberations today?" The African American woman asked.

"Rose, everything went well, I held my position on Slavery." Andrew said.

Rose's face went flush in disappointment, but she knew she could not convince Andrew to change his position on slavery.

Apophis could tell that Rose wanted their secret to be public, especially for the sake of their children. Apophis took control of Andrew's body.

"What is for dinner, Rose?" Apophis asked.

"Ribs and Potatoes." Rose answered.

"Let's eat." Apophis said

"The table isn't set yet." Rose said.

"No, need for a tablecloth, just plates, forks, and napkins. What will we drink?" Apophis said.

"Well, we can drink red wine or water." Rose said.

"I'll have red wine." Apophis said walking to the dining room, while Rose went back to the kitchen for cups to place on the table.

Bastet appeared to Apophis, while he was still in control of the body. Bastet gave Apophis a glare of disapproval.

Apophis ignored her, knowing she was standing there being only visible to him and no one else in the room.

Rose walked into back in the dining room, she called for the children to come to dinner.

The children came running to the dinner room. The children sat down at the table. Rose served the food, then sat down at the table. Apophis was about to eat the food, as he was reaching for the food on his plate, Rose smacked his hands. She gave him a look of disapproval as if he knew better. Bastet was chuckling in the corner of the room.

"Andrew, you know we always say Grace before the meal." Rose scorned him.

Apophis looked at Rose confused.

"Sorry, I had forgotten." Apophis lied.

"Let us bow our heads and say grace." Rose said grabbing Apophis's hand and her children's hands making a circle around the dining table.

Apophis winced as Rose started to recite the Christian prayer. Apophis felt a burning feeling as the blessing at the table was being said. Bastet raised an eyebrow and twitched her tail. Once the prayer blessing was finished Apophis was a bit dizzy from the burning pain.

"How about next time we just eat next time, without the blessing of the food?" Apophis asked.

Rose was confused at the strange request; she had a puzzled look on her face.

"It is tradition and the proper way to do things the Christian way." Rose said.

"Well, let's take a break from the blessing before the food for next time." Apophis said beginning to eat his food in front of him.

Rose looked shock at Apophis, she knew she wasn't smart enough, let alone even educated enough to understand people's behavior, in fact she was only taught to talk, no reading or writing, let alone any other skills. She felt weird with the request.

Rose took a deep breath.

"We don't need to bless the food next time." Rose said beginning to eat her food.

Everyone was eating their meals, when suddenly there was a knock at the door.

"Who could that be at this hour?" Rose said starting to get up to get the door.

"No, eat your food, I will answer the door." Apophis said getting up to open the door.

Apophis walked out of the dining room into a long hallway that led to the front door. When Apophis got to the door, he opened the door, at the door was congressman Seth. Apophis recognized him.

"Andrew, is this a bad time? I really need to speak with you." Seth said.

"Well, we are sitting down for dinner. Could you come back later?" Apophis said.

"We? Who is 'we'?" Seth said barging in through the door.

Seth made his way down the hallway, making his way to the dining room. When he made it to the dining room, he was beyond shocked when he saw Rose and her children at the table.

"I am surprised that you let your slave woman and her children to dine with you, I personally force my slaves to eat in another room away from me, the low life creatures." Seth said knowing he was insulting Rose.

Apophis got offended that Seth called Rose a 'low life creature'. Apophis does not see her as a low life, in fact back in the time, his slaves ate with him and were well respected, as well as treated more like equals not just as slaves.

Apophis had them as soldiers, just like his children were bred as.

"Well, she is my wife, and these are my children. I love them from the bottom of my heart." Apophis said.

At first Seth laughed thinking it was a joke, but then he realized it was serious, his eyes widen in disbelief.

"Well, I just realized that I forgot something, I need to go." Seth said speeding out the door like he was being chased by a lion.

Rose looked at Apophis in discontent.

"WHAT THE HELL?! YOU TOLD ME NOT TO TELL ANYONE AND YOU TOLD ME WE WERE A SECRET!" Rose screamed at Apophis at the top of her lungs.

"I don't want to keep it secret anymore." Apophis said calmly.

Rose was filled with many different emotions from rage to relief then concern.

After 30 minutes of trying to calm Rose down, they went back to eating their dinner.

Meanwhile, across town, Seth was speaking with other town folks to include friends of Andrews. They all couldn't believe that Andrew had done something so filthy and distasteful, not to disrespectful of the culture and social norm of the time.

They all were plotting to murder the family by burning the house down. A sort of cleansing of the unpure so to speak.

After the family ate, Apophis took the four children to bed and tucked each one into their separate beds.

Shortly, after the children fell asleep, Apophis and Rose went to the bedroom to get ready for bed.

"Andrew, since our secret is out, let's celebrate by making love." Rose said.

Apophis agreed.

While Apophis and Rose were about to make love, a sudden crash came through the front windows. Apophis and Rose both panicked at the sound.

"What the hell was that?" Rose said.

"Stay here, let me check something." Apophis said looking out the window.

Apophis saw outside a crowd of people carrying torches, axes, and pitch forks, he saw that the whole group of people surrounded the entire house and perimeter around the house to prevent escaping out the back and sides of the house. Flames began to spread from the front of the house towards the bedrooms.

Multiple crashes kept coming back-to-back and the flames kept getting stronger.

"Get the children, now." Apophis demanded as Rose and him ran out of the bedroom.

They went and woke all the children up, the flames were spreading faster and every inch of the place, there was not a place untouched by flame. Outside you could hear chanting "Burn the disease."

Apophis and the family were trapped inside one of the rooms in the back of the house. Apophis went to the window, immediately he saw his children that he saw them standing in the crowd, they were watching the tragic event that unfolded before them. They had been witnessing to many such events over the Millennia. No one else could see Apophis's children, they were like ghosts to the surrounding crowd.

Within a matter of minutes, Apophis was back in the Eternal Blackness. Apophis's flesh still was stinging from the burning, but he doesn't remember hearing screaming from the children as they burned alive. Nor does he recall anyone telling each other they love one another as they were engulfed in flame. The crackle of the flames were far too loud to hear anything of the sort.

Apophis stared across the never ending black abyss that he was floating in, he felt a terribly strong pain in his heart, he remembered the joy he once felt thousands of years ago before the banishment. He remembers watching his children growing at a fast rate, three times the speed of any normal human child. He was shocked that he saw them in that crowd that was burning his last host's home.

No one in that crowd, but him saw his children. They were surprisingly had the ability to be like ghosts. He knew his children are the immortal ones compared to regular humans.

Apophis could only imagine what they were thinking, as they witnessed Apophis burn in that house. The last time, Apophis's children had seen him in a host that was a slave, they were not happy then as they were now seeing Apophis, since they are holding a grudge against him and believing he had abandoned them, thanks to the council's doing. This act of betrayal that the children of Apophis believed happened to them is truly nonexistent, but they will not listen to reason, they will continue to believe they were both betrayed and abandoned by Apophis. Their hatred will grow and grow to the point that, they made it their mission to find Apophis, every Halloween, no matter what host he was in and take revenge, but there could be other opportunities other than Halloween, even though that is the day they are the strongest.

Apophis knew this, but he couldn't figure out on how to ensure that they could understand that their hatred was misplaced. How could he get them to understand that he is not the enemy, and that the Council is the true enemy?

While Apophis was contemplating in his solidarity, he was summoned to the council chamber. He looked in front of him, hovering above him, sitting there all noble and smug was RA, the sun god of Egypt, the main hawk head. He was sitting there in his throne glaring at Apophis with a smirk on his face. Sitting next to him on his right side was his son Horus, and on his left side was Hathor, his wife and daughter. They all glared down upon Apophis, as did the rest of the Council.

Apophis, you have broken a quite many rules, you were not supposed to take full control, you are not tasked to bring happiness to anyone whether it be host or host's family. You're a prisoner in a sentence of exile within a host. You are meant to suffer and learn from punishment." RA roared down from his high throne.

The great God Thoth, stood there with his papyrus, recording this summoning, which entailed everything that was said by RA and everything that everyone he has done, he is the scribe of the gods, record keeper of all things, he has the head of a crane headed god. He oversees wisdom and knowledge.

Apophis knew Thoth sided with RA on everything that RA declares.

"May I impose more punishment length?" Hathor suggested.

The entire Council Chamber roared in a chatter across every pantheon of all Gods and Goddesses. RA grinned sinisterly.

"SILENCE EVERYONE!" RA shouted.

Silence fell as fast as a stone across the entire chamber.

"Apophis, you will be in this banishment for the rest of time." RA declared.

Apophis's eyes grew large as he let out a large gasp at the ridiculous thing, RA had declared. Before Apophis could protest his defense, he was sent to a new host.

Unknown host #17

Hello,

It is me, Apophis again. Yes, as you could see if I did something right or wrong, the Council only sees it all wrong. They have a very unfair system of "justice" if you could call it that. Honestly, the council themselves have been causing far more damage to the world, yet they don't see it that way. Anyway, this next host that we are going to write about will pick up during the civil war. This next host is going to go by Robert, please enjoy the stories of each host.

-Apophis

Apophis woke up in a white sheet tent, laying on a cot with twelve other cots in the tent with him. Apophis looked at what clothes his host was wearing, a blue uniform. Apophis was unaware of what the color signified, let alone the year, Apophis got up and put on his host's boots that were next to the cot. Apophis got up from the cot and walked towards the opening of the tent.

Once outside of the tent, Apophis saw a large military encampment in an open field, surrounded by forest. There were over 5,000 soldiers in this battalion.

Apophis was amazed that this country was at war again. He had no idea that the war was against itself. Apophis walked around the camp for a bit until a colonel came up to him.

"Private Robert, have you recovered from you sniffles from the medical tent already?" The colonel asked.

Apophis was caught off guard with the question, so he played it off.

"Yes, in fact, I was wandering what year is it? Also, where are we? And I forgot your name, what is it?" Apophis asked.

"Have you been hit in the head in there? You forgot to address me as 'sir', and it is 1862, we are just outside Virginia, my name is colonel Smith." Colonel Smith said.

"I'm sorry, sir. I must ask why we are stationed out here?" Apophis asked.

"You must have really hit your head. We are at war with the states to the south of us over slavery and other political issues that are above our pay grades." Colonel Smith said.

Within moments, Apophis was pulled into the darkness in the back of the host's mind. Apophis looked around confused, until Bastet appeared to Apophis.

"What do you want, feline?" Apophis said in annoyance.

Bastet's tail twitched at the tone of Apophis's voice.

"Well, hello to you Apophis, I'm sure you are wondering what is going on, well after your last host. This country began to go to war against itself, you didn't help things last time either." Bastet said.

"Well, I was already caught up with half of that." Apophis snapped back.

Bastet glared at Apophis for a moment with her emerald, green feline eyes. Then she continued.

"You will bare witness to the warring nation, as brother kills brother, ripping the nation apart to the brink of failure. You have no power to influence this war to stop." Bastet warned with a strict tone in her voice.

"Was this war part of the Council's game?" Apophis asked, already knowing the answer to the question.

Bastet remained silent; she knew the truth. Bastet turned into the darkness and disappeared, leaving Apophis alone.

Apophis knew that Bastet knew the true motive of the Council. The Council loves human suffrage and pain, they have been doing this since mankind began walking the Earth. The top two favorites of the Council of human suffrage are war and disease.

Apophis knew that he was a pawn in the Council's little game. The sad part is the Council's game is playing out not just here on Earth, but on millions, possibly billions of other worlds.

Meanwhile, back in the earthly realm of Apophis's host, Robert was coughing profusely and releasing large amounts of yellow mucus mixed with some blood. Apophis saw that his host had an infection, a Bronchitis infection.

Unfortunately, Apophis cannot heal infections as severe as this one. Apophis looked into the memories of the host, that the infection was going on for three days, unfortunately, with the cold nights and damp field the camp was setup in, as well as the medicine of the time wasn't advanced enough to fight an infection as severe as this.

Robert was sent back to the infirmary tent; Apophis took over feeling the full strength of the sickness. Every inch of the body was infested by the infection, making the muscles weak. Apophis could feel the host body had hours left.

A nurse laid Apophis down in the closest cot, that was empty. Apophis laid there in the cot shivering and shaking, the body had a high temperature. The nurse pulled a blade out of the field medical kit and began to cut Apophis's host's arm and other parts of the body. This process was called "Bloodletting." This process is where they medical professional cuts you in the affected areas to release "bad blood" in the body. The process was popularized from the ancient Greeks who believed the human body was made up of four humorous or fluids that needed to be balanced out by cutting one effected area, in the process of bloodletting.

The sharp blade cut deeply into the flesh, The pain was unbearable, Apophis felt every cut from the sharp blade. Apophis felt that the host's body was far too weak, it suddenly gave up on life. Apophis was back in the Eternal Darkness in a matter of seconds.

Apophis floated there in the blackness; he placed his hands on his face covering his eyes. Apophis shook in rage from dealing with each other these deaths was the worst part of this banishment.

Apophis knew that this banishment was going to drive him insane one of these days, he saw no way out of this cycle. His mental strength will break one day, even the strongest tree in the forest falls sooner or later. 17 separate hosts, 17 separate deaths, each one painful much like the last. Apophis wondered how many more lives, how many more deaths or centuries would it be before he would lose his mind completely. Being in the Eternal Darkness, there is no warm or cold temperatures, no light or air flow, but Apophis could feel a cold chill of dread running down his spine.

Anubis walked into the darkness, where Apophis was at. Apophis saw him walking up, walking all firm and noble towards Apophis.

"What do you want, you smelly hound?" Apophis said rudely.

"I just wanted to let you know that in the earthly realm in the country of America has been at war with itself for a year, killing thousands more of soldiers and innocents from burning towns and homes." Anubis said.

"Why are you telling me all of this?" Apophis asked curiously.

"I wanted you to know that these were sacrifices that the council deems acceptable, to keep the balance of the universal scales and power they hold." Anubis said.

"I don't need you to tell me how powerful the Council is. I don't fear them, the accused me for something they did thousands of years ago, that is why I am here in this banishment." Apophis snarled.

Anubis got quiet and felt a deep cold shock run down his spine. Anubis knew that Apophis was right that the Council had framed him to get him out of their way. Anubis knew that the Council would frame anyone that is deemed a threat to their main plans. Anubis turned quickly without saying a word and left Apophis alone once more.

Uknown host #18

While Apophis floated there in the darkness, thinking about what Anubis had just said to him, then within a matter of moments Apophis was engulfed in a flashing white light, being transported into a new host. For this host, we will call him Robert, as well.

Apophis saw that he was in another encampment, but this time these soldiers had gray uniforms, this camp was in the middle of the woods as well as the last one he was in. The only other difference of this encampment was that these soldiers appeared more exhausted and malnourished, of course both camps had inadequate medicines.

Apophis walked around the camp; he walked up to a soldier that appeared to be in control of the camp.

"Sir, what year is it?" Apophis asked.

"Lieutenant Robert, must have been one hell of a hangover, huh?" The soldier asked.

"Yes, sir." Apophis said.

The soldier laughed and scoffed at Apophis.

"Well, it is 1863, I know we have been at war for these two long years. Soon we will end those Yankees." The solder said with high confidence in his voice.

"Who are you, sir?" Apophis asked.

"I'm Colonel Johnson, I hope you remember next time, instead of asking three times." The Colonel said with frustration in his tone.

Apophis realized that his host had a drinking problem and a very forgetful memory. Apophis let his host take back control of the body, he wanted to observe what his host will do, and he wanted to see the intact memories of this host.

Robert, the host, felt disoriented, extremely confused on what had just happened, as far as he knew was, he was asleep. He decided to go to the nearest town to go to the local bar to drink. Apophis went to the host's memories, he saw thar the host already fought and survived 12 battles. Apophis learned that his host's birth name is Alexander, he changed it to honor his idol Robert E. Lee. Apophis saw that the reason his host changed his name is because he was bullied all his life for the name and because of a murder he committed to one of the bullies.

Robert was a citizen in the northern state of Pennsylvania, after the murder he defected to the southern state of Florida, then he changed his name then. Three years later though, the war had broken out. The drinking is to numb the guilt for murder he committed.

While Apophis was looking through the memories, Robert was walking through the town, with the cool evening air hitting his face, until he came to a bar. He went up to the bartender and asked for a rum bottle, he paid with a $20 gold piece. He began drinking the rum and becoming plastered drunk and uncontrollable. While he was drinking a beautiful brunette woman walked past him in a red and blue dress. The dress was poofy and large as for the fashion of the time was. The dress made the woman have a large buttock and large breasts from the corset she wore underneath the dress. This attracted Robert, as both her and him began to leave the bar unaware of one another, Robert began to follow her like an animal stalking its prey.

Robert followed her outside the bar and down the street, when the brunette looked back and noticed Robert was stalking her, she began to pickup speed trying to run, but the dress was too cumbersome from its impractical design of the time. She tumbled to the ground from the dress. Robert saw an opportunity to snatch her up and drag her away. Robert bent down and picked her up. He threw her over his shoulder. The woman a bit dazed from her tumble, when she started to wake up from her daze. She panicked.

"What are you doing to me? Where are you taking me?" She protested.

Robert dropped her from his shoulder, then he pulled a cloth from his pocket and wrapped it around her mouth to keep her silent, he then lifted her back over her shoulder. He took her to the nearest abandoned building, the building was dark, musky, damp and rotting away.

The woman began to panic more, she began to squirm to try and get herself free from her attacker. Robert threw her with a brut force to the wood floor. The woman landed with a thud that knocked the air out of her. The woman was winded and in sheer pain. Robert began to rip her dress, but the woman who was still in her dazed state tried to kick him, but Robert got more angered at the struggling victim. Robert looked around until her found a loose brick on the ground, he picked it up and began beating the woman over the head with the brick. The woman died from the six blows to the head, Robert of course still in his drunken state was unfazed by it.

Robert removed the dead woman's clothes and began to rape her newly dead corpse. Apophis saw this and was disgusted at such sickness. Apophis had never thought of having sexual relations with a dead body, Apophis knew that this was one of the sicknesses that the Council had instilled in the human condition.

Once Robert had finished, he pulled a match out from his pocket, lit the match and threw it on her deceased body. The dress was still touching the dead body as it ignited slowly burning, the flames were not as fast do to the lack of combustible liquid on the dress.

Robert walked out of the building as it began to go ablaze, the rotting wood was easily burned. Robert begun to make his was back to the camp.

Meanwhile, Apophis was wishing for this host life to end, he had seen this disgustingness plenty of times. Apophis was ashamed of the humans, but he was more ashamed of the Council for creating this condition in the human race.

After fifteen of a walk, Robert had made his way back to camp, he was stumbling to make his way back to his tent, that he collapsed from his drunken state right in the middle of the camp, falling fast asleep.

The next morning, Robert was still dead asleep in the middle of the camp. His commanding officer saw him laying there asleep. His commanding officer went over to him, got close to Robert's ear and shouted so loud that the whole camp could hear it all around.

"WAKE THE HELL UP, YOU LAZY SLUG!!" The commanding officer screamed and kicked Robert hard in the back, much like a horse that kicks to awaken Robert.

Robert awoke with the sharp pain in his back, he stood up and grunted from the pain. Apophis felt the full blow Robert had taken in the back, chest and stomach; he took full control since Robert still was incoherent from the alcohol.

"I am sorry, sir. I mistakenly fell asleep here. I lost my way last night." Apophis said still wining in pain from the painful kicks.

"Lost your way, retard? Well, give me sixty laps around the camp." The commanding officer demanded.

"Yes, sir." Apophis said preceding to start running.

With every breath Apophis took was like sharp knives in his host's chest. The kicks have caused some internal bruising. Apophis tried hard to complete the runs around the camp, but this body wasn't in the greatest of shape, on top of all the pain was too great, that Apophis's host's body collapsed from the pain and exhaustion, he blacked out.

Within a matter of what felt like six hours, Robert awoke inside the infirmary tent, Apophis was out in the subconscious part of Robert's mind. Apophis was observing everything from what Robert saw now.

A camp doctor came up to Robert and informed him that he needs to rest for three days. Robert understood that his body was in terrible shape, he felt the sharp pain with every breath. He had no memory of what had occurred other than the night before. After that was a complete blur to him.

Meanwhile, outside the infirmary tent, over in the command tent, the generals of the camp were making plans to invade Gettysburg, Pennsylvania in three days, they hoped to win the battle of Gettysburg. Across to the northern side of the city of Gettysburg, the Union army was planning and preparing to move out to defend Gettysburg.

As the three days by like a flash of light from the sun. Robert recovered quickly; the army was preparing to march onto Gettysburg.

Robert was suited up and got in formation.

The march began, a ten-mile march, everyone was nervous to fight in the hopes that this would be the last battle to win the country.

Bastet joined Apophis to watch the march. Apophis knew that the rest of the Council was watching these events unfold from high above, like a kid with a magnifying glass, watching ants.

When the army entered the city of Gettysburg, shots begun to fly from both sides, Robert tried to avoid the gun shots and cannon fire, but within a matter of twenty minutes, stray cannon fire took out a building of bricks and stones that came crashing down on top of Robert crushing him flat.

Apophis felt brief pain, then it was back in the Eternal Darkness, alone once more.

Apophis sat there in the temperature less blackness, he thought to himself on what he could do to end his suffering. He knew he could not simply commit suicide like normal humans can. He wished deeply to be free and to fully regain his powers once more, one day soon.

Bastet walked into the darkness towards Apophis. Bastet had a strange confident look on her face, Apophis was concerned on why that was.

"What is with the look on your face?" Apophis asked with concern in his voice.

Bastet noticed the tone of his voice.

"Well, I'm in just a confident mood, I feel confidence is something to be joyous about. I won't tell what I am confident about, it is a secret." Bastet fiendishly with a smile on her face.

Apophis grew uneasy from the look on her face.

Unknown Host #19

Before Apophis could say anything, a flash of light engulfed Apophis sending him to his next host.

When Apophis had arrived in his new host, he saw that he was at a racetrack for horse jockeys. Apophis looked around when he saw a ticket in his hand that said "Jockey number 12". Apophis figured that his host was a gambler. He saw that the ticket said the year 1867, on the top of the ticket. The world hasn't changed much, the world was still recovering from the extensive years of war damage.

For this story of this host, we will call this host, James.

Apophis switched control with his host, heading to the bad of the mind to learn and observe this host.

Twenty seconds, after switching with the host, the announcer at the racetrack had announced that the horse jockey number 12 had won the race. Apophis could hear excitement screams exploding everywhere. The host went to the redemption window to claim his winnings.

"Your name, sir?" The window clerk asked.

"James." James said.

"You have won $36 million dollars on your $200 dollar bet on number 12. Congrats on your winnings, sir." The clerk said counting out the money for James.

Apophis was shocked at how lucky his host was, it was unbelievably impressive. Apophis knew that this host must have some sort of deal going on other than this, he must be one of the Council's pawns that are blessed with such great luck, but then why would the Council put his in this host, if they intended him to be punished?

Apophis went to his host's memories, he saw that his host was extremely lucky, there were other memories showing how risky the bet from across his lifetime, winning all the bets. There were bets with knives to shooting bets, these were forcing the odds against life, especially his own life.

Later that night, James made it home. When he got home, he walked through the front door with a large grin on his face, he went into the living room. Sitting there in a chair was his blonde wife, she had beautiful white pearl skin, with sapphire blue eyes. She heard her husband walked; she turned her head towards him.

"Hello, honey. How were the horse races?" His wife said getting up to greet him.

James smiled and opened his arms to hug his wife, she walked into his arms.

"I won $36 million dollars from my bet." James said.

His wife pulled back slowly from him, until her face was fully visible, her eyes grew large at the news, she smiled in excitement.

"I am glad how lucky you are. What are we going to do with our winnings?" She asked.

"Well, let's invest some, save some and I have other bets I would like to make to win more money." James said.

His wife walked over to a small table that a small leather book sat on the table with a Quail feather pen in an ink jar next to it. She opened the book, grabbed the Quail feather, dipped it three times to get a good amount of ink, before writing down the date and the amount of money won for the day.

James walked over to look, there were 36 pages filled with his winning in the last two months, turns out he has 150 journals filled with records of his winnings.

Twelve minutes later, someone was banging at the front door. James' wife went to the front door. The second she opened the door, a masked gentleman burst through the door, knocking her down to the ground by the sheer force of the door being forced opened. The masked gentleman grabbed the dazed lady on the ground by the hair, then he grabbed a small wooden bat and hit her over the head, knocking her unconscious.

James heard the commotion from the front door.

"Hon, are you okay?" James said.

When he didn't get a response, he went to the front door, hiding behind a wall in the entry way, the masked gentleman hid there waiting for James to come down the hallway.

As James entered in the entry way, he saw his wife knocked out on the floor.

"Honey, what happened?" James asked rushing to her aid.

James didn't notice the masked intruder behind him as he was trying to awaken his wife. The masked intruder crept up behind James and got close to him to hit him over the head, but thankfully the floor creaked giving away that someone was behind James. James turned around, seeing the intruder, he stood up fast to fight off his attacker.

In a matter of minutes, three other masked intruders entered in the open front door, following behind the first one.

During the struggle with the first one, James was hit over the head with a blunt object by one of the other intruders, causing James to black out and fall to the ground.

Apophis thought he was back in the Eternal Darkness, until a few minutes later, when James woke up, James looked around panicking, he felt his arms were bound to his wife. They were back-to-back, sitting in chairs, tied up. The intruders were standing across from James and his wife. The leader of the group was pacing back and forth, swinging his small bat.

"What the hell do you want from us?" James asked panicking, struggling to get loose from his bounds.

"We want the money that you won today." The leader of the intruders said still pacing and swinging his bat.

"You won't find it here; I sent it to a large vault in a bank." James lied to the intruders.

The leader scoffed at James and shook his head.

"I know that you are lying, how about a wager? If you win, we will release you, and we leave peacefully, and penniless. If we win, we get all the money, and you will keep your lives." The leader said.

"Fine, let's wager, all or nothing." James said frighted and knowing he couldn't resist a wager.

The leader of the intruders grinned mischievously. The leader knew that James couldn't resist any wager.

"Good, here is the wager, if you can hold a lite dynamite stick your rectum before it blows you to bits, you will win." The leader said showing the dynamite stick to James.

What James didn't realize was the fuse wire was shortened to a ten second delay. Apophis didn't notice the shortened wire either.

The other three intruders, stood there silently, until one of them was instructed to untied James. James walked up to the leader of the intruders, looked at him dead in the eye.

"Drop your pants and undergarments." The leader of the intruders demanded.

James undid his pants, pulling them and his undergarments down to his ankles. He bent over a chair that was in the room, like the position like when someone is going to either wipe someone's butt or have anal sex.

One of the intruders went up to James with the dynamite in his hand, he placed a jelly onto the dynamite stick and slowly shoved the stick into James's anal hole. James felt the dynamite stick stretch open his anal hole, the pressure was uncomfortable, the rectum tried to resist, but it made its way into the rectum, just enough to hold it in place.

James felt nervous and embarrassed with his ass and penis exposed to the intruders, the strange thing was is that his penis was fully erect.

The leader of the intruders noticed and laughed at the sight of the erect penis.

"So, you enjoy things in your ass?" The leader of the intruders laughed as he lite the fuse.

James and his wife were sweating profusely out of nervousness, the stick felt uncomfortable being placed inside James' rectum. Apophis felt the pressure from the stick as well.

Within a matter of seconds, the stick blew up, killing James, his wife and the intruders, little did they know that the uniform factory behind the house had a natural gas leak which caught on fire killing 120 workers in the explosion.

Back in the Eternal Darkness, Apophis felt a split open from the death he had just experienced. Apophis saw Bastet, Anubis, and Nut standing there in front of him laughing at him, he then realized that Bastet knew he was going to experience his host's death in such a horrid ridiculous way. That was why she acted so smug beforehand. This greatly enraged Apophis, because it was not just a punishment banishment, but a way to humiliate him as well.

From this point on he knew The Council already knew what ways his hosts were going to die. Apophis planned to find a way around the rules that The Council put in place to prevent him from doing anything.

"That was hilarious, the way your host died." Bastet said still laughing her ass off.

"His face right when he was blown to bits was priceless." Anubis barked out of laughter.

"Your host really reached for the stars through his ass." Nut said busting a gut referring to how she is the goddess of the sky.

"You guys are Bastards; don't you realize that? That man was innocent. Plotting his death for your amusement is uncalled for." Apophis scolded.

"Well, we did get 120 others dead too. They are perfect entertainment." Anubis said all proud at what The Council had done.

"Mark my words, I'll..."

"You will what?" Bastet interrupted Apophis midsentence.

Three seconds later, before Apophis could say anything, he was in the middle of The Council chamber, the sounds of laughter filled the entire chamber. They were all laughing at what had just transpired to Apophis's host.

RA stood all proud from his mighty throne, beak glistening, eyes sharply staring down from on high.

"Apophis, you were going to say something that Bastet has informed me that we all in The Council should hear, please enlighten us." RA roared down with his thundering voice.

Apophis looked all around him, then he mustered the strength that he had to declare what he wants to say.

"I was going to say, you guys are cruel and mark my words, I will destroy you one day soon!" Apophis shouted.

There was a moment of silence, until RA and the other member of The Council bursted out in a horrendous laugh. They took Apophis as a joke, this further enraged Apophis.

"You cannot destroy us, you are weak, powerless to do anything to harm us." RA roared down, now angered at what Apophis had said.

Unknown host #20

"Your absurd thought of destroying us is a form of blasphemy, for that you are going to your next host now, no waiting in the darkness." RA declared, with a swing of his arm and a flash of light sent Apophis away.

This next host we will call Javier.

Apophis woke up in the middle of a busy street, with people preparing for an incoming storm. They were shoving passed a confused Apophis, who was trying to figure out where he was at.

"Hey, asshole. Get out of the middle of the street!" screamed a passerby, who shoved roughly into Apophis.

Apophis started walking, he got to the other side of the street. On the other side of the street, Apophis found himself now on, he found a newspaper stand. Apophis walked up to the newspaper stand, he picked up a newspaper which read "1870". The storm everyone preparing for was a tropical storm, but it wasn't named at the time. Apophis realized that it was three years after his last host, the transition period between hosts is rather confusing for Apophis, since being in the Eternal Darkness for a few minutes is the equivalent of years on the Earthly plane. Even a few minutes in the Council Chamber for a few minutes could be different in the time for the Earthly plane.

Hello, it is Apophis again. Yes, the time perception as you call it or rather time dilation, is very different within the Eternal Darkness and Council Chamber. These are on their own separate planes of existence. These planes are far from what human consciousness can reach, The Council purposefully did this to keep your minds from reaching it. The Planes your minds can reach is a lower plane, they ensured your version of the metaphysical realm is limited, anything beyond that is their realm. Yes, they can come and go as they please from these realms, but not for you.

-Apophis.

Apophis decided to let the host take over, while he went to the back of the host's mind to learn more about him.

When Apophis entered the back of the host's mind, he saw that the host's name was Javier, a Frenchman, known for his cons on unsuspecting people.

Apophis went to watch what his host was heading to do. He watched as Javier scammed tourists and local people that his oils would help them be safe from the on coming storm. As well as protect their property from damage during these uncertain times. Of course, humans fell for it during their times of panic. People were buying out the oils left and right, within minutes, Javier had amassed himself quite a large fortune from scamming.

Once he had amassed his fortune, satisfied with the results, he began to pack up his stand and head home. Once he made his way to a brick building, he went down some stairs that were leading down to the basement of the building. Javier lived in the basement of the building, he entered into his home, and put his stand and extra unsold oils away. He pulled out a large wooden box with a lock on it, he unlocked the lock, opened it, there was a huge pile of money that he had accumulated. He pulled out from a bag he carried on his back, pulling the money he gathered that day, placing most of it in the wooden box, locking it back.

Later that night, after the entire city was evacuated, Javier left his home to wonder the streets, he had broken into a liquor store, taking all the whiskey that he could carry. Within 12 minutes, the first drops of rain started to pour, as Javier was leaving the liquor store, during the walk home, Javier was drinking the whiskey beginning to get drunk, the strong winds begun as Javier stumbled his way home.

When Javier got home, he was already on his third bottle of whiskey, causing him to be too drunk to care about the storm. He laughed stumbling and slipping down the stairs, Javier wasn't coherent enough to realize the flooding had begun. He entered into his home, falling flat on his face on the already wet floor that was filling slowly with water, but Javier was too drunk to care, he fell asleep. Apophis felt the air becoming thin, he felt the lungs of the host beginning to fill with water. In the city, there was flooding with water rushing into Javier's home in the basement.

Within a matter of moments, Apophis was back into the Eternal Darkness. Apophis was coughing and gasping for air as a side effect of the death of the host. Apophis tasted salt water in his mouth.

There Apophis sat alone in the blackness, once again feeling that painful loneliness, the dreaded chill running through his body. He knew soon he would start the cycle over once again and again, but never knowing if it would end. Could the cycle be broken? Loneliness is the true torment of all, no one to see or hold, just that empty abyss. The Council knew this, that's why they enjoy isolating people from people that care about them.

The ultimate way to hurt someone is to make them feel lonely and darkness will grow within them.

Apophis felt a deep loneliness, he wondered how much longer it would take to be out of what seems on being an eternal banishment. He sat there in the darkness alone, staring out into the uninviting, uncaring black abyss, which is enough to drive anyone insane within a matter of moments.

Bastet walked into the blackness; Apophis stared at her with a cold stare.

"What do you want feline?" Apophis said with irritation in his voice.

Bastet just stared right back at Apophis with a blank, emotionless look for a moment.

"I've come to see how your mind is holding up. Many have gone insane by now begging for all this to end." Bastet said.

"How many have you sent into this banishment?" Apophis asked.

Bastet stayed silent, indicating many thousands or more have been banished such as Apophis, but the were weak and begged for their punishment to end.

How does one get out of Banishment, such as this, you may ask?

Well, you are taken to the Council Chambers where the Council would bring in the same crystal that they originally banished you with. The Crystal would essentially tear your soul to shreds when it is at full power, basically killing you permanently.

Apophis knew that this would be an outcome that he would not want, he knew he was stronger than the others that were banished before him and during his current banishment. Apophis vowed to not let the Council win.

Unknown host #21

Within a matter of moments, Apophis was transported into a new host. For this host we will call this host Altan (AL TN).

Apophis saw he was inside a beautiful palace, there were many servants all around, everywhere Apophis had walked, they all greeted him, he came across a beautifully carved golden throne. Apophis was amazed with what he saw, he wished he could stay in this host longer, but he knew it would soon die like all the others. Apophis walked over to a papyrus type paper on the wall, it was a type of calendar, the calendar read "1872" for the year.

"My Emperor Altan, I am here to report that a farm near the border is under threat of invasion." An advisor said holding more scroll types of paper.

Apophis turn to look at the advisor.

"Sent the Army to defend this town and farm, right away." Apophis ordered the advisor.

"Yes, sire." The advisor said bowing and turning to leave to let a military advisor to send the Army to the farm and town by the border.

Apophis let his host take control again, he went to the back of the mind to rest since he wasn't fully ready to be in control since he still had some trauma from the last host.

Later that night, Apophis saw that his host was sick from E. Coli bacteria, which was slowly killing his new host. The Emperor requested his servants release fecal matter into a plate for the night for the emperor to eat. Apophis learned that this host loved eating human waste, learning this revolted Apophis, he watched as his host was eating the human waste.

While Apophis's host was enjoying his human waste, his Army was slaughtered at the border to include all the towns folk and six other towns that are in the area. The enemy was on their way to the palace. The Emperor's power was weakening right under his nose since the invading force was slaughtering everyone in its path.

Apophis could feel the warm feces pass the lips of the host and go down into the stomach. It was nauseating to witness and feel it. Apophis was overwhelmed by the smell and the taste of the feces. Apophis was too distracted to realize that his host's body was failing from eating the human waste.

By the sixth bite into the waste, Apophis's host began to vomit up the waste with blood. The room began to spin along with more and more violent vomiting progressed.

Within a matter of two hour, Apophis was back in the Eternal Darkness. Apophis was confused because he didn't feel any side effects, let alone he didn't realize host his host died. Bastet walked into the blackness.

"What happened? How did I end up back here this time?" Apophis asked Bastet in confusion.

Bastet looked deeply into Apophis's eye.

"Well, your host was violently vomiting from the E. Coli. He caused his body to dehydrate, which caused him to black out and then his death shortly after. It was painless." Bastet explained.

Apophis tried to process this; he shook his head.

"Dehydration isn't much of an honorable death." Bastet said.

"I didn't feel the death this time." Apophis said.

Bastet smirked at how funny this death was, then she turned and left Apophis alone in the darkness.

Sitting there in the blackness, Apophis was drawing his plans to take his revenge upon the Council. He was planning on finding a weapon to fight and destroy the Council, but where would he find such a Weapon?

Uknown host #22

While in the middle of his thoughts, a flash of light engulfed Apophis transporting him into a new host.

For this host we will name him George, this host is quite a player, in the sexual sense.

Apophis awoke in an office, that was beautifully decorated, with the best most expensive wood desk of Mahogany. Apophis had not seen such a beautiful wood piece such as this or that he noticed at all. Apophis stood up from the leather chair that was in the office, it was a hard back leather chair, swivel chairs were more of a later part of the next century. Apophis began to walk around the office, he saw a window, that observed some kind of factory floor. He walked over to the window, he looked out the window, he saw assembly lines for weaponry.

Apophis was amazed at how the weapons were being created on assembly lines, since in his time, it was only a small group of Smithers and metal workers to create the weaponry of Ancient Egypt. These assembly lines had multiple people working to build and put together the modern weapons that these countries use for war, home defense and the like. Apophis loved to see this impressive sight. There were enough weapons in this factory to supply a large Army.

Apophis turned towards the wall that was on the right of window. On that wall there was a calendar that read "1875". Apophis realized that the length of time he was in the Eternal Darkness was three years earth time. Apophis decided to learn more about this host through the memories.

Before Apophis went to look at the memories, a gentleman employee walked into the office.

"George, sir. There is a representative here from the Military." The gentleman said.

"Send them in, I will speak with them." Apophis said.

The gentleman turned and left.

Apophis quickly switched with his host. A second later, the representative walked into the office.

"Hello, George. I wanted to mention an order of quadruple the amount this month, compared to last month." The Military representative said.

George's eye grew large, he has never had such an order in all his years of operation. George collected himself.

"The cost of the will quadruple that of the standard amount." George said.

"We can pay for it, in fact, I have the payment with me now." The representative said setting out six brief cases of money on the desk that him and his fellow associates were carrying. They each opened each one of the cases on top of the wooden desk. Each case revealed stacks of neatly place currency, money. George grinned his greedy grin at the sight of the amount of money.

"That will certainly cover the cost of it, we will have your ready in a week." George said.

"We will need it in three days, can you have that done in that timetable?" The representative said closing the cases of money.

"Yes, we will work in triple shifts." George said.

The Representative thanked George and went on he way. After he left George went to the balcony that was above the factory floor.

"Attention everyone, I won't be shutting down the factory floor for the next three days. Our biggest customer has requested quadruple their normal order. I will give everyone $2 dollars extra bonus per hour for the triple shifts. You can get two lunches each day, since you will get the bonus shifts." George declared off the top of the balcony.

His employees began working on the order, they had a great incentive for what was a lot of money at the time.

While his workers worked their fingers to the bone and around the clock, George left to go to the local bar, he left his floor manager in control of operations, while he stepped out.

Apophis saw that George wasn't the family type, unlike some of his previous hosts. He was a hustler in the game of love, he was very unstable when it came to his romantic life, he prefers sexual relations with random people.

George went up to the bar, and the bartender went over to him.

"What can I get you to drink?" the bartender said to George.

"I'll have whiskey with three glasses." George said handing the bartender a one-hundred-dollar bill.

The bartender took the money, the turned, pulling out three glasses and putting a full bottle of whiskey on the bar counter. George poured himself a cup of whiskey, then suddenly a woman and a gentleman came up to George, Apophis could see that George knew both the blonde woman and the brown-haired gentleman.

"Hello, George. Are you ready for some fun tonight?" The woman said kissing his neck.

Oh yes, I am ready for our expedition tonight." George said getting lustful.

"So are we, let's go somewhere private, but first let's get something to eat." The gentleman said grabbing George and the woman's hands.

Apophis was confused on what his host George meant by "Expedition". So, Apophis went digging through the memories, but he would soon regret what he might find.

Meanwhile, George and his companions went to a restaurant to eat. Apophis soon found out what the word "Expedition" word meant. Apophis saw that his host eats out both male and female anal regions known as analingus.

Apophis winced at the disgusting sight that he saw in the memory, he knew that was going to happen again tonight. Apophis dreaded seeing this and knowing that he would taste everything, since he is connected to the host.

When George and his companions got done eating, they went to his house. When they arrived at his home, they went inside and began to kiss each other and remove their clothes. The gentleman reached around from behind grabbing ahold of George's penis beginning to stroke it, while at the same time he grabbed the woman's breast. Apophis watched in disgusted, to Apophis this wasn't normal ways to make love.

The woman got down on her knees and began to suck both the guy's penises, as both guys were kissing each other. George began to kiss both the woman and the gentleman at the same time, he kissed and licked both their bodies, he sucked both of their bodies, when he got to their anal regions, he began to lick, kiss and suck to outside, working his way to the holes. The woman and gentleman both moaned in pleasure. George spread both their cheeks open, beginning to lick and suck the anal holes.

Apophis felt nauseous at the fecal taste in his mouth, the smell was unbearable, both anal regions were not cleaned properly, unfortunately for the time hygiene wasn't very good.

The sexual encounter lasted two hours, with both gentleman fucking the woman at the same time, her vagina stretched with the two penises inside it. The woman gave George head, while his ass was being pounded by the gentleman, Apophis was shocked at the feeling and sight of all this, his body was felling weird and defiled as this sexual encounter happened.

After the sexual encounter happen, Apophis learned that his host lived with his companions. They shared the same bed together. While his companion's slept, George got up and got ready to go back to his factory, he kissed both of his companions on the forehead before leaving.

When he arrived at the factory, he went to his floor manager.

"What is the status on the customer's order?" George asked.

His floor manager turned to him.

"Well, sir. We are about a fourth of the way done with the order. Of course, this is to be expected since we have never worked at this rate before." The floor manager said.

"A fourth?" George said disappointed.

George went up to the front of the factory floor.

"Excuse me, everyone. I wanted to say, if you work faster and I will give you an extra dollar each." George said.

While George was saying this to his employees, a fire broke out in the lower levels, due to his over worked employee falling a sleep at the smoldering station.

After George gave his short speech, he went to his office. Just before he could sit at his desk, an explosion happened that shook the factory, causing George to fall to the floor.

"What the hell?!" George said running out of his office.

When he got to the bottom of the stairs another explosion hit shaking the stairs causing George to tumble down the stairs, Apophis felt the sharp pain from the tumble. George stood up and looked around seeing that all his employees running, and flames were rising high.

"What is going on?!" George shouted.

Everyone was running out of the factory as the flames were roaring through the factory.

George tried to evacuate the factory, but before he could get halfway through the factory floor, when the roof collapsed on top of him. Crushing and burning him alive. Apophis felt the blistering burning feeling until the final moments of the host.

Within moments later, Apophis was back into the Eternal Blackness once again.

Apophis still felt the blistering burning feeling from being burned alive. He tried to focus all his energy he had to get rid of the feeling. Being in the blackness, focus has come easy to Apophis. He has spent a lot of time in the blackness that he has learned to focus.

Bastet walked into the blackness, her face was firm and neutral. She examined Apophis, noticing he was still feeling the leftover connection to that last host.

"Apophis, you need to know that you are stronger than anything I've ever seen before." Bastet said.

Apophis was confused that Bastet said that to him, he raised an eyebrow.

"Why do you say this?" Apophis asked with curiosity in his voice.

Bastet knew that she better be careful at what she says. The Council listens to everything and sees all. If she slips up and encourages Apophis, she will be banished like him.

"Well, I just thought you looked gloomy, so I lied to get you in a better mood." Bastet lied.

Apophis knew Bastet was lying by the tone of her voice. He knew that she needed to be very cautious at what she says because the Council hears everything, she could get hurt if she says the wrong thing.

Bastet knew that Apophis was back to himself, she turned without saying a word to Apophis leaving him alone in the darkness.

Unknown Host # 23

This next host we will call Joseph, let us begin.

Within a few moments of Bastet leaving Apophis alone in the darkness, a flash of light engulfed Apophis transporting to him to his new host.

When Apophis awoken, he was in a strange place, the surroundings were even more alien to him, than the others he had been in. There were temple structures that he thought he recognized because of the architecture was similar to those in the Council Chamber. Apophis looked closer at the people and the statues that were all over the place, then it suddenly dawned on him. He was in the country that the Hindu Gods ruled. How could he not recognize them at first? He knew the Hindu Gods had chosen this place, but he wasn't in their people. He looked at the skin, it was white, and the clothes were different, he was in a soldier's body from the British Empire.

Apophis reached into his host's pocket and pulled out a piece of paper that read "Orders: Stationed assignment for Joseph in India, year 1880."

Apophis was shocked that the paper said "India". India of all places in the world, Apophis never liked it, even during his time. The Egyptian Pantheon section of The Council has always had issues with the Hindu Pantheon, just like other Pantheons such as the Greek and Roman Pantheon. But India was the strangest and never truly fell in line with the Council's rules. Of course, a great number of them have been banished for their disobedience.

Apophis felt even more out of place, Apophis saw how filthy this country was, none of the people were being taken care of well. Apophis could see how the British army could invade and conquer this country, so easily.

"Captain Joseph, you are invited by the Emperor at the Palace for a grand ball tonight." A native Indian servant said leading him to the Palace.

Once they were inside the Palace, Apophis saw beautiful golden fixtures everywhere. Apophis couldn't believe his eyes. Suddenly, he was pushed out of control of the body. He was dazed in the blackness in the back of the host's mind.

"Don't get any ideas, you cannot be in control of these riches. You know the rules." Bastet said swinging her tail.

Apophis stood, turning to have a view threw the host's mind. Apophis watched as his host walked through the Palace with the servant leading him to the Emperor's chambers.

Once they arrived at the door to the Emperor's chamber, the servant open the door, there in his throne was a thin gentleman that had a crown of gold and silver on top of his head, encrusted with large Diamonds, Rubies, Emeralds and Pearls on it.

Apophis could feel that his host was beginning to sweat, his greed kicked in at the sight of the precious stones on top of that crown. Apophis saw thoughts form of his host imagining on wearing that crown, as well as imagining stealing the crown.

The Emperor stood from his throne and started to walk towards Joseph.

"Hello, Captain Joseph. I have considered your countries' offer and I will let your country have control of the land and the mines, as well as other resources in my country as long as you give us a cut of the profits." The Emperor said.

"Yes, I will send the message along to my countries leaders." Joseph said.

"It is settled then; I invite you to a grand feast and stay in my Palace for the night." The Emperor said with open arms as if he was going to give Joseph a hug.

In fact, he did hug Joseph, Joseph felt awkward about the hug, but he knew it was their customs.

At the dinner table that night, there was fruits, beef, duck, goat, and so much other foods that the Gods and Goddesses would enjoy the feast.

Apophis was amazed at the amount of food there was. Apophis decided to take control of his host and eat food, because he wasn't sure when he would see such a feast again. Apophis began to grab foods from all over the table and fill his plate. He knew that it had been a few hosts since he has had such a delectable feast.

The Emperor looked at the plate that Apophis had filled us and was surprised at what he saw.

"You must be hungry from your long journey." The Emperor said noticing how fast Joseph was eating, unknowing that it was Apophis in control.

"Yes, military rations are not as delicious as your food, sir." Apophis said playing the part.

"Enjoy yourself here, make yourself at home, here in my palace." The Emperor said graciously.

"Thank you, sir. In fact, where shall I be sleeping tonight? If you don't mind my asking. I've traveled a long way." Apophis said.

The Emperor clapped his hands, spoke in his native language directing his female servants to lead Joseph to his guest chambers.

Apophis stood up from his chair and followed the servant girls to his chambers. After about five minutes of walking down a beautiful hallway, Apophis and the servant girl arrived at the guest chamber. When they walked into the chamber, the servant girls began to undress, Apophis was pulled out of control of the body, Bastet had pulled him back.

"You are not to have sexual pleasure!" Bastet exclaimed.

"Alright, I get it. All part of the banishment." Apophis said.

"Yes, part of it, you are not supposed to enjoy your punishment. The Council wants me to make sure that you suffer." Bastet said whipping her table back and forth aggressively.

Joseph was dazed for a moment, a bit confused on where he was and why he was with two beautiful women and why were they undressing him.

Joseph noticed the jewels around their necks and hands. Each women began kissing his legs making their way to his penis, kissing and licking it. Each women sucked Joseph's penis as they stroked and got undressed. Joseph enjoyed the euphoria rush from the pleasure on his penis that he was receiving. Once the women were completely naked, the led Joseph to the bed and laid him down with his erect penis. One of the women got on top of Joseph's penis inserting it into her and began to grind on him, while the second woman put her vagina in Joseph's face, riding his face as Joseph was eating her out. Apophis could smell the sweet scent from the servant girl, it was mesmerizing. Joseph was sucking and licking the vagina. The two women kissed each other, and both moaned in pleasure.

Bastet grinned knowing as long as Apophis watched, his punishment will become more antagonizing, but it is only limited.

Each women took turns riding and thrusting on Joseph's penis and his face. The pleasure Joseph felt was intense, unlike anything he ever experienced before. The sexual act lasted an hour before the women left the room.

Joseph, who had enjoyed himself immensely, was still plotting on stealing the crown from the king that night.

Apophis was annoyed with all the bad people he has had been put in, but he knows The Council loves to add extra torment to those they despise most, being that Apophis was on the very top of that list.

Joseph planned to sneak out of the room and steal the crown around 2 a.m.

Later that night, while the entire Palace slept, Joseph slowly and quietly stepped out of his room, he went down a long hallway with his backpack was on his back. The Palace was all around decorated beautifully, Joseph noticed that there were Emeralds and Rubies in the walls of the Palace. He pulled his knife out and began to pull them out of the wall. As he pulled a bunch of the precious stones out, he still made his way to the crown room.

When he got to the crown room, he saw the crown on a pedestal. He walked up to the crown and picked it up and quickly put it in his backpack. Joseph took off running as quickly and quietly as he could. When he came to a window, he climbed down scaling the wall of the Palace.

Once he hit the ground, he made his way to the nearest dock to depart on a ship.

While Joseph was making his way through the city, some street urchins blocked his way.

"Get out of my was, sir." Joseph demanded.

"No, I need your money." The street urchin said pulling out a knife.

"I have no money, leave me be." Joseph said backing away.

"That's fine, I'll take your fancy looking bag around your shoulders there." The urchin said cornering Joseph against a wall.

Before Joseph could respond or defend himself, the urchin thrusted the entire 16-inch blade into Joseph's throat.

Apophis felt the stabbing, which blocked the airways of his host. Two minutes of consciousness was long enough to watch the thief take the bag with the crown and jewels.

Moments later, Apophis was back in the Eternal Darkness.

Apophis just floated there in the blackness, with a cold burning stare on his face. The thoughts ran through his head. He was under a lot of stress from jumping from one host to another, death after painful death, each more painful than the last.

Unknown host #24

While Apophis was deep in his thoughts, the bright flashing light engulfed him. Apophis was sent to another host body.

Apophis had awoken in a room, that was the size of ancient Pyramid chamber, it was surrounded by vaults. Apophis walked around and examined the vaults; he saw a sign the read "United States of America Mint."

Apophis walk further down the long hallway until he got to an office space.

For this host we will call him Jack, this is the best name for this host.

Apophis opened the office door and saw a desk with a newspaper on the desk, Apophis went over to the paper and picked it up, the year on the paper was "1883".

Apophis decided to let his host take control. Apophis went to the back of his host's mind.

"What the hell? I was just auditing the vaults." Jack said out loud to himself.

Jack pulled several small bars of gold out of his pockets, which were all once ounce bars. There were 24 of these bars, in total it was the equivalent of a 24-ounce bar.

Apophis saw in Jack's memories that Jack had dark intentions with that gold, he wanted to steal it, he had already stolen a total of $299 million dollars' worth of gold.

After Jack's shift was over, he left his job with the stolen gold in his briefcase, he went to his secret location in the middle of the woods, where he kept his secret stash of stolen gold.

When he arrived at his secret stash location, he opened the wooden door that led to an underground hole, it was a about the size of a small Egyptian tomb. Jack opened his briefcase, pulled out the small bars of gold and placed it in a large trunk with the others in this tomb mound.

Jack had seven other trunks full of one ounce gold bars. He placed the last of the bars he took in the trunk, he knew that would be enough for him to retire comfortably.

Once he had put the bars in the trunk, he closed and locked the trunk, then he stood up and left the tomb mound. He walked out of the wood onto a road, where Jack was hit by a speeding horse drawn carriage, which left him within an inch of death, but for Apophis, it was already too late, he was sent back to the Eternal Darkness.

Bastet Appeared to Apophis, she saw the confusion on Apophis's Face.

"What happened?" Apophis asked.

"Well, the impact from the carriage, technically killed your host for three minutes, that is why you are back here so soon as it did. Your former host is still alive, but you will be moving on to a new host." Bastet said.

Bastet explained that in the future for that host. Jack was to die in a hurricane in 1927 in Haiti. He did however, manage to get all of his stolen gold out of the country and retire comfortably there.

Apophis was shocked to hear what happened to that host.

Bastet and Apophis both set there floating in the empty blackness for a moment staring at each other.

"How would I know that The Council would free me, once this is all over?" Apophis said breaking the silence between them.

Bastet hesitated for a moment afraid of whether or not to tell Apophis the truth that he would never be free from this banishment or lie to him telling him he will be free, but not to harm after the banishment would end. Bastet was nervous on what to say.

In a moment, a flash of light engulfed Apophis to a new host.

THE NEW MILLENNIUM

Unknown host #25

This host we will name Jessie, this host will be in a soda factory.

Apophis awoken inside a room filled will forty or fifty cot beds. The air smelled musky loud production sounds, shouting all around.

Apophis looked down at his hands, he saw how small they were. Apophis realized that he was in a child's body.

Apophis stood up and walked out of the large room and discovered that he was in a soda factory, a drink that he was unfamiliar with, but the glass bottles resembled that of alcohol bottles.

Apophis walked aimlessly around his new surroundings. He was learning his new environment, until he was noticed by the floor manager.

"Jessie, you seem lost, do I need to remind you that you are on bottle filling duty?" The manager said with irritation in his voice.

Apophis complied walking back to where the soda was being bottled, but quickly turned to the manager.

"What year is it, sir?" Apophis asked.

"1886." The manager said not paying much attention to the question.

"Thank you, sir." Apophis said letting his host have full control again.

Apophis went to the memory section of the child host. Apparently, this was a 12-year-old child, who has been spitting in soda bottles for two years, he has been downing this for fun.

He knew that people would not notice saliva in their soda because the soda masks it, especially, on hot days. Every three days he spits in six bottles of soda.

Apophis was disgusted but had to laugh because he knew full well on how unobservant people can be.

While Apophis was going through the memories, his host was at his work station spitting in six soda bottles like he usually did.

While this was going on, down in the basement of the factory, by the furnace, the workers forgot to close the coal furnace door. So, a hot piece of coal fell out of the furnace on to the pile of coal stacked next to the furnace.

With no one there to supervising the coal and the furnace. The stacks of coal went ablaze in a fire. The fire engulfed the entire basement within a matter of minutes. The flames quickly spread up to the main factory floor.

When a passerby finally noticed the fire, it was already too late. The factory was halfway destroyed by the time it reached Jessie and Apophis.

When Jessie heard the screaming and the smell of the smoke from the flames, he took off running trying to escape the flames, but his little legs could only carry him so far, just before a metal beam fell on top of him, this instantly killed him, but for those few seconds before the beam hit. Apophis heard explosions and screams of agony throughout the factory.

Within a matter of mere seconds, Apophis was back in the eternally damning blackness. This time none of the other Gods or Goddesses came to visit him. Not Bastet nor Anubis, nor anyone else.

Apophis was sitting there in the blackness utterly alone with his thoughts. His thoughts ran wild as if they were sentient in themselves.

Apophis thought he should just give up, that there was no point in fighting The Council, they are many, he is but one. There is no one who can help him fight them.

Unknown Host #26

For this host, we will call him Steven.

In that moment, when Apophis was deep in thought, a flash of light transporting him to another host appeared.

Apophis had awoken deep inside a coal mine; he looked around his surroundings. The mine was deep and dark.

"Steven, I am not paying you to be in Fairyland! Get back to work or I'm docking your pay." The foreman shouted.

"I'm sorry, sir. I'll get back to work, but could you tell me what year it is?" Apophis said.

"Too many drugs again? It's 1892, you got to lay off the cocaine. It is messing with your mind." The foreman said with a smug sound in his voice.

Apophis realized that he was a few years, until the new century. Apophis went into the back of the mind, letting the host take back control.

Steven felt dizzy and strange, he felt like he had blacked out for a moment. He resumed his duty in the mine for another four hours.

During that time, Apophis learned that this new host was a heavy drug user. He wondered if he could change that.

When Steven finished his shift, he proceeded to leave the freshly dug mine shaft he was located in. He went into an elevator loaded with other workers.

"Damn, what a hard day, I can't wait to get home, eat and have a beer." One of the workers in the elevator said.

Once the elevator reached the top of the shaft, everyone started to step off the elevator. They all went to a locker room that was above the mine.

Steven on the other hand went into the foreman's office. As he entered the office trailer, there sitting on the desk was a box full of cash.

Steven saw that the box wasn't locked up, he looked to check to see if the foreman was on his way back to his office, when he noticed that the coast was clear. Steven quickly opened the box that was filled with a total of about $2000 dollars or more. Steven quickly pulled out $500 dollars out of the box and put it in his pocket and closed the box as fast as he could.

Steven quickly left the foreman's office than rushed to go to the locker room. Apophis saw in disbelief on what had just happened. Another greedy host, Steven apparently has done this before on several occasions.

Apophis saw over 300 memories of his host stealing $500 each time.

"How could he not get caught in the act?" Apophis wondered to himself.

Apophis watched as his host went to the bar to spend the full amount he had just stolen. He bought food and drink for every single person in the bar since being extremely affordable (being it is lower amounts compared to today).

Apophis heard the bartender say that a steak was a dollar. Apophis was amazed at the price, he remembered when in his time, a steak costed whole twelve bars for a nice piece of steak.

Apophis watched and tasted every sip of alcohol and the meat that passed through the host's lips. Apophis knew that it was torture for him to just watch and get little tastes of meat.

Apophis took control of the host's body; he began to devour any meat he could order.

Once he finished, he left the bar and went to the host's home. He found out from the memories.

Apophis felt the host began to feel nauseous, he stopped halfway before heading to the front door of the bar and vomited all over the floor.

The crowd exclaimed "Ewww!" and began to laugh.

When Apophis finally made it outside, the warm air slapped him in the face. He turned to walk down the street three blocks.

After twenty minutes, Apophis came to a small bungalow with a beautiful garden in the front. Apophis was amazed at the beauty of the garden, he originally thought that the home would be run-down and filthy because he is a coal miner, his judgement was wrong.

Apophis proceeded to walk up the pathway in the front of the bungalow. Apophis pulled out the keys to the home, as he got to the front porch, he saw the beautiful Oak front door, which was beautifully crafted.

Once Apophis got the door opened, he walked inside and went straight to the bedroom. Apophis saw no sign of a women or children in this home. This home was neat and clean though.

Turns out Steven was a neat freak and loved to garden, his hobby makes him happy.

When Apophis came to the bedroom, he discovered that Steven was a worshipper of Bastet. He saw a large ancient Egyptian statue of Bastet sitting in the corner of the room with candles around it.

"Great, another worshipper of Bastet." Apophis thought to himself.

The second he turned around he saw laying on the bed, petting a cat was Bastet. Bastet saw the look of shock on Apophis's face, while she was petting the beautiful long-haired cat.

"What? You don't like that statue of me?" Bastet said sarcastically.

"No, it's not that. I just didn't know he was a worshipper of yours. The memories of that are blocked to me." Apophis said.

"Yes, they are, thanks to me. I didn't want you to know just yet until now." Bastet said with a large grin on her face.

Bastet watched Apophis like a scientist studying a specimen. Apophis laid on the bed, Bastet laid next to him.

"Why are you laying next to me?" Apophis asked.

"I want to. I feel like you have been alone all this time." Bastet said rubbing her tail on Apophis's leg.

Apophis pushed her tail away and scoffed at her.

"Why are you rejecting me?" Bastet asked.

"I have no attraction to you, feline. Isn't this against the rule with The Council? Aren't you not supposed to have sexual relations with the banished?" Apophis said with irritation in his voice.

"No, it isn't against the rules. Ra has fucked many of those that are banished." Bastet said.

"Lokk, I don't want sexual relations with you, feline." Apophis said.

Bastet sat up with tears in her eyes.

"I am sorry for trying." Bastet said quickly getting up and disappearing into the darkness of the darken room.

Apophis laid there on the bed staring up at the ceiling until he fell asleep.

The next day, Apophis's host was back in control. Steven sat up on the bed, groaning in pain from a very massive headache. He got up off the bed and stumbled to the bathroom and began to vomit. The hangover, he was experiencing was terrible.

After 30 minutes of vomiting, (mostly dry heaving), Steven got ready for work. He began to wash his face. Apophis never understood the point of this strange ritual. Apophis sat back there in the back of the host's mind wondering why Bastet would try to seduce him.

Apophis never saw a point to why any of the Gods and Goddesses should find attraction to one another, he knew he wouldn't have created his army if he slept with one of the Goddesses back before the banishment.

After steven got ready for work, he walked over to the Bastet statue and prayed next to it.

Once he finished praying to Bastet for good health and protect as well as prosperity, he got up and went to the kitchen to get his lunch ready for the day. Apophis scoffed at the prayer he had heard. The only thing Bastet could protect is her own ass, Apophis laughed at the thought of that.

Steven got a sandwich and apple ready for work, once his meal was ready, he quickly got out the door. He waved down a horse drawn carriage to go to the mine.

Once he got to the mine, he quickly made his way to the locker room, put his lunch pail way in his locker, then he punched in for work. He went to the mouth of the mine, making his way to the elevator near the opening of the shaft. When he got to the bottom of the shaft, he turned his lantern on and went to his station, beginning his work.

After 30 minutes into his shift, blasting began in the above chambers of the mine began. The shaft started to shake from the explosive vibrations, Steven did not stop working, since he was used to the explosions.

By the twelfth explosion, which was the largest of them all. The entire mine shaft began to collapse on top of Steven, which began to crushing him instantly.

Apophis was back in the Eternal Darkness after the feeling of being crushed by over a thousand pounds of coal and stones on top of his host.

Apophis felt that cold chill running down his spine, he wonders what the next death in store for the next host is few hosts, or many more host.

After what felt like an hour a bright flash came and Apophis was transporting him to the Council Chambers. Right in the middle of the large chamber, he stood there looking all around. Every one of those Gods and Goddesses were chatting loudly amongst themselves.

Once Ra appeared out from behind a door that was behind his throne. His muscular physical appearance with his bird head, his beak glistened from the chamber's bright light.

Ra looked down on Apophis from his high post. He looked at him in disgust.

"Apophis, you have broken many rules in your time in the hosts. For this, your banishment will be extended for another 12,000 years." Ra commanded.

Apophis's face was in shock, everyone chattered louder. Ra raised his hands to silence the chamber.

Unknown Host #27

"We will send you away now." Ra boomed down.

Before Apophis could say anything, a flash of light engulfed him. Apophis awoke in a host that was sitting in an office. Apophis felt rage, he knows The Council is a threat that must be dealt with.

But now was not the time to deal with the Council, he wasn't strong enough to take them on. The Council has been in power for billions of years, since before the time of dinosaurs. Their power spans across countless worlds in the Universe.

Hello, Everyone

Yes, The Council has controlled your world for billions of years as well other Alien worlds, you thought that you were their only play things? No, The Council has influence across many worlds. I know that this story of mine is massive, we will break this up into a couple of books. Thank you for sticking with me this far.

-Apophis

Apophis hoped for a great help one day to defeat The Council.

After Apophis switched his focus from The Council to his new host. For this host we will call him Seth. Apophis got up from the chair he was in at the desk. He went over to the calendar hanging on the wall and saw that the year was "1896", and the name on the plate on the desk read "Seth".

Apophis walked back over to the desk and saw plans to buy 236 acres of land in Texas. His host would spend $90 million on land there.

Bastet appeared out of nowhere. She walked towards Apophis.

"Sorry, I saw what The Council agreed upon." Bastet said.

"I don't want to hear from you Bastet." Apophis snapped.

"Don't blame me, I was not involved in that meeting with the others. I was tending to my cats." Bastet pleaded to her defense.

"I don't want to hear your pathetic excuses." Apophis said.

Bastet stood there silent, twitching her tail. Apophis scoffed at her.

"Fine, I forgive you, stop guilt tripping me." Apophis said.

Bastet grinned, hugged Apophis, then turned and disappeared.

Apophis let his host take back control. Seth was feeling dazed and confused on what had just happened.

"Jimmy, do you the file on the resources on the Texas land?" Seth said over a pipe speaker, that was devised to communicate through to the other person, it is similar to an electronic speaker without electricity.

"Yes, sir. I will bring it to you." Jimmy said.

"Also bring me the file on the Wyoming land deal as well." Seth said.

Apophis went through his host's memories, he saw that his host believed that Wyoming had oil, but the research of the spots in the middle of Big Horn Basin and the land outside the Wind River Basin has no oil. The spots were purchased by Rockefeller and other companies.

Seth went through his paperwork, he then turned his attention to the bottom left drawer of his desk, he opened it and pulled out a medium sized cloth bag, along with a match and some cigarette paper. He opened up the bag, pulling out a hand full of Marijuana. He laid out the cigarette, set a bit of Marijuana on it, rolled it, then he lit it, take a long drag from it.

Apophis tasted it in his mouth. Apophis took control and put the joint out. Apophis has never tasted anything so awful in his thousands of years of life. Apophis did not like the taste of it, his host got buzzed from the Marijuana.

Apophis knew The Council created such an awful tasting plant. The Marijuana is a poisonous plant created to cause issues within the mind and soul of the users. Purity is destroyed once you consume such a nasty drug. Bastet appeared to Apophis laughing at him.

"What is this disgusting plant?" Apophis asked.

"Oh, Marijuana, the Greeks created it to cause mental anguish within it's users. Ra approved of it's creation about one thousand years after your banishment began." Bastet said.

"That is just typical of The Council. Why haven't the other hosts that I've been in not used this drug?" Apophis said.

"They were wiser not to use it." Bastet said.

Apophis took the cloth bag and threw the Marijuana bag deep in a trash bag and down the trash shoot.

"Awe, what a waste." A voice said from across the room.

Apophis and Bastet turned to look who was speaking. Standing in front of the door was Zeus, the head God of the Greeks pantheon. Apophis felt a burning hatred rise inside his heart.

"What are you doing here, you disgusting Greek?" Apophis demanded knowing he insulted Zeus.

Zeus stared at Apophis, then he said, "I am here to see your reaction to my invention and gift to Mankind." Zeus lied through his teeth.

"Don't give me that 'Gift to Mankind' bullshit. You and I both know that it is a poison to bring damage to Mankind." Apophis said.

Zeus remained quiet and turned, then disappeared, knowing that Apophis was right. Bastet looked shocked at Apophis for putting Zeus in his place.

"What was that about?" Bastet asked.

"Well, he is a dumb Greek God that needs to learn his place." Apophis said.

"Wow, you have shocked me, Ra was right and so was the rest of The Council to fear you." Bastet said.

"Fear me? They just don't like anyone who doesn't follow like a sheep to their rule." Apophis said sternly.

Bastet's tail fluffed up in tension, she got offended at what Apophis just said, being called a "sheep" hit her hard.

Apophis noticed the look on her face.

"What? Did I hit a nerve with you?" Apophis said.

"Yes, you offended me." Bastet said.

Bastet then turned and left Apophis alone. Apophis knew that Bastet was easily offended, but he does consider Bastet, Anubis, and many other members of The Council were just sheep, fearing if they were not following the rules of The Council that they would end up banished.

Thousands alongside Apophis have been banished throughout time, there is always a chance of running into another banished member, but if they banded together. They would surely suffer being brought forth in front of The Council and their essences stripped and destroyed by the original Crystal Pyramid that banished them. This would be the ultimate death of all, a fate that none of the banished would want.

Seth's assistant walked into the office with the file on Wyoming.

"Is everything alright,sir?" the assistant asked setting the file on the desk.

"Yes, everything is well, just eager for this deal to go through." Apophis said pretending to be his host.

"That's good, sir. Also don't forget about the card game tonight." The assistant said reminding him.

"Ah yes, the card game. I will be there." Apophis said.

Apophis switched with his host. Seth felt dazed as if he was just woken from a sleeping state. He pulled his pocket watch out and saw it was time for the card game.

Seth rushed out the door of his office. Seth quickly stopped by his company's vault to withdraw the deed to his company just in case he ends up short on his bets during the card game.

By the time, Seth made it to the local bar, where he did his card games, it was already pitch-black outside. As he entered into the bar, he saw a table of his normal card playing buddies sitting there. He walked up to the table, when one of the guys turned to him as he sat down at the table.

"Welcome Seth, we are ready for the card game." The gentleman said passing out the cards.

Seth placed $20 dollars in the middle of the table.

Apophis saw the game of cards as a waste of time and a huge bore. He went to see what he could find outside of the body through astral travel. He came across a museum.

As Apophis entered the museum, he went to the Egyptian exhibit. He found a spell book that was on display called "The spells the ward off Apep".

Apophis was pissed to see this on display. The Council created this to humiliate Apophis, his other name was Apep. Apophis knew that these spells were to hurt him if he ever returned, and The Council was prepared. Also these were more humiliation instead of harming him.

Three hours went by until Apophis went back to his host. He was seeing other things The Council had influenced people to create to humiliate him and create an image of an evil being. This in turn caused Apophis to be enraged.

By the time Apophis returned to his host, Seth had a pistol in his mouth.

Apophis looked in the memories and saw that Seth had lost his entire fortune and his company.

Before Apophis could see the rest of the memories, Seth pulled the trigger on the pistol. Apophis felt his head split open and then in a matter of seconds it was back in the Eternal Darkness once again.

Apophis floated there in the Eternal Darkness, still feeling the painful effect of the ball bullet from the pistol. Apophis's thoughts started to wonder. He thought of how much longer the brutal torturous banishment would truly last. The wait in the blackness is one of the worst moments in the banishment.

Within a few moments of being in the blackness, a flash of light engulfed Apophis. What Apophis thought he was going to be in a new host, but he looked around and saw that he was in the middle of The Council Chambers again.

Rage was bubbling up inside, Apophis couldn't control it.

"WHAT THE HELL DO YOU WANT FROM ME NOW?!" Apophis screamed which echoed throughout the chamber.

Ra stepped out on to his ledge, looked down upon Apophis, cracked a mischievous smile, knowing he finds joy in causing Apophis pain, suffering and slowly making him have mental anguish.

"Apophis, we in The Council have decided to let you know that you will be in a new century that will be many surprises in store for you." Ra said.

Apophis scoffed at what Ra had said.

"I know you really brought me here for your entertainment!" Apophis shouted.

Ra's grin grew bigger as he released a very loud and sinister laugh.

A flash sent Apophis out of The Council Chamber.

TO BE CONTINUTED IN BOOK 2

<u>Message from the Author:</u>

I hope you enjoyed this book, I love astrology and knew there was not a book such as this out on the shelf. I love metaphysical items as well. Please check out my other books:

-Life of Government Benefits

-My life of Hell

-My life with Hydrocephalus

-Red Sky

-World Domination:Woman's rule

-World Domination:Woman's Rule 2: The War

-Life and Banishment of Apophis: book 1

-The Kidney Friendly Diet

-The Ultimate Hemp Cookbook

-Creating a Dispensary(legally)

-Cleanliness throughout life: the importance of showering from childhood to adulthood.

-Strong Roots: The Risks of Overcoddling children

-Hemp Horoscopes: Cosmic Insights and Earthly Healing

- Celestial Hemp Navigating the Zodiac: Through the Green Cosmos

-Astrological Hemp: Aligning The Stars with Earth's Ancient Herb

-The Astrological Guide to Hemp: Stars, Signs, and Sacred Leaves

-Green Growth: Innovative Marketing Strategies for your Hemp Products and Dispensary

-Cosmic Cannabis

-Astrological Munchies

-Henry The Hemp

-Zodiacal Roots: The Astrological Soul Of Hemp

- Green Constellations: Intersection of Hemp and Zodiac

-Hemp in The Houses: An astrological Adventure Through The Cannabis Galaxy

-Galactic Ganja Guide

Heavenly Hemp

Zodiac Leaves

Doctor Who Astrology

Cannastrology

Stellar Satvias and Cosmic Indicas

<u>Celestial Cannabis: A Zodiac Journey</u>

AstroHerbology: The Sky and The Soil: Volume 1

AstroHerbology:Celestial Cannabis:Volume 2

Cosmic Cannabis Cultivation

The Starry Guide to Herbal Harmony: Volume 1

The Starry Guide to Herbal Harmony: Cannabis Universe: Volume 2

Yugioh Astrology: Astrological Guide to Deck, Duels and more

Nightmare Mansion: Echoes of The Abyss

Nightmare Mansion 2: Legacy of Shadows
Nightmare Mansion 3: Shadows of the Forgotten
Nightmare Mansion 4: Echoes of the Damned
The Life and Banishment of Apophis: Book 2
Nightmare Mansion: Halls of Despair
<u>Healing with Herb: Cannabis and Hydrocephalus</u>
<u>Planetary Pot: Aligning with Astrological Herbs: Volume 1</u>
Fast Track to Freedom: 30 Days to Financial Independence Using AI, Assets, and Agile Hustles
<u>Cosmic Hemp Pathways</u>
How to Become Financially Free in 30 Days: 10,000 Paths to Prosperity
Zodiacal Herbage: Astrological Insights: Volume 1
Nightmare Mansion: Whispers in the Walls
The Daleks Invade Atlantis
Henry the hemp and Hydrocephalus

10X The Kidney Friendly Diet
Cannabis Universe: Adult coloring book
Hemp Astrology: The Healing Power of the Stars
Zodiacal Herbage: Astrological Insights: Cannabis Universe: Volume 2
<u>Planetary Pot: Aligning with Astrological Herbs: Cannabis Universes: Volume 2</u>
Doctor Who Meets the Replicators and SG-1: The Ultimate Battle for Survival
Nightmare Mansion: Curse of the Blood Moon
<u>The Celestial Stoner: A Guide to the Zodiac</u>
Cosmic Pleasures: Sex Toy Astrology for Every Sign
Hydrocephalus Astrology: Navigating the Stars and Healing Waters
Lapis and the Mischievous Chocolate Bar

Celestial Positions: Sexual Astrology for Every Sign
Apophis's Shadow Work Journal: **:** A Journey of Self-Discovery and Healing
Kinky Cosmos: Sexual Kink Astrology for Every Sign
Digital Cosmos: The Astrological Digimon Compendium
Stellar Seeds: The Cosmic Guide to Growing with Astrology
Apophis's Daily Gratitude Journal

Cat Astrology: Feline Mysteries of the Cosmos
The Cosmic Kama Sutra: An Astrological Guide to Sexual Positions
Unleash Your Potential: A Guided Journal Powered by AI Insights
Whispers of the Enchanted Grove

Cosmic Pleasures: An Astrological Guide to Sexual Kinks
369, 12 Manifestation Journal
Whisper of the nocturne journal(blank journal for writing or drawing)
The Boogey Book
Locked In Reflection: A Chastity Journey Through Locktober
Generating Wealth Quickly:How to Generate $100,000 in 24 Hours
Star Magic: Harness the Power of the Universe
The Flatulence Chronicles: A Fart Journal for Self-Discovery
The Doctor and The Death Moth
Seize the Day: A Personal Seizure Tracking Journal
The Ultimate Boogeyman Safari: A Journey into the Boogie World and Beyond
Whispers of Samhain: 1,000 Spells of Love, Luck, and Lunar Magic: Samhain Spell Book
Apophis's guides:Witch's Spellbook Crafting Guide for Halloween
<u>Frost & Flame: The Enchanted Yule Grimoire of 1000 Winter Spells</u>
<u>The Ultimate Boogey Goo Guide & Spooky Activities for Halloween Fun</u>
Harmony of the Scales: A Libra's Spellcraft for Balance and Beauty
The Enchanted Advent: 36 Days of Christmas Wonders

Nightmare Mansion: The Labyrinth of Screams

Harvest of Enchantment: 1,000 Spells of Gratitude, Love, and Fortune for Thanksgiving
The Boogey Chronicles: A Journal of Nightly Encounters and Shadowy Secrets
The 12 Days of Financial Freedom: A Step-by-Step Christmas Countdown to Transform Your Finances
Sigil of the Eternal Spiral Blank Journal
A Christmas Feast: Timeless Recipes for Every Meal
Holiday Stress-Free Solutions: A Survival Guide to Thriving During the Festive Season
Yu-Gi-Oh! Holiday Gifting Mastery: The Ultimate Guide for Fans and Newcomers Alike
Holiday Harmony: A Hydrocephalus Survival Guide for the Festive Season
Celestial Craft: The Witch's Almanac for 2025 – A Cosmic Guide to Manifestations, Moons, and Mystical Events
Doctor Who: The Toymaker's Winter Wonderland
Tulsa King Unveiled: A Thrilling Guide to Stallone's Mafia Masterpiece
Pendulum Craft: A Complete Guide to Crafting and Using Personalized Divination Tools
Nightmare Mansion: Santa's Eternal Eve
Starlight Noel: A Cosmic Journey through Christmas Mysteries
The Dark Architect: Unlocking the Blueprint of Existence
Surviving the Embrace: The Ultimate Guide to Encounters with The Hugging Molly
The Enchanted Codex: Secrets of the Craft for Witches, Wiccans, and Pagans
Harvest of Gratitude: A Complete Thanksgiving Guide
Yuletide Essentials: A Complete Guide to an Authentic and Magical Christmas
Celestial Smokes: A Cosmic Guide to Cigars and Astrology

Living in Balance: A Comprehensive Survival Guide to Thriving with Diabetes Insipidus

Cosmic Symbiosis: The Venom Zodiac Chronicles

The Cursed Paw of Ambition

Cosmic Symbiosis: The Astrological Venom Journal

Celestial Wonders Unfold: A Stargazer's Guide to the Cosmos (2024-2029)

The Ultimate Black Friday Prepper's Guide: Mastering Shopping Strategies and Savings

Cosmic Sales: The Astrological Guide to Black Friday Shopping

Legends of the Corn Mother and Other Harvest Myths

Whispers of the Harvest: The Corn Mother's Journal

The Evergreen Spellbook

The Doctor Meets the Boogeyman

The White Witch of Rose Hall's SpellBook

The Gingerbread Golem's Shadow: A Study in Sweet Darkness

The Gingerbread Golem Codex: An Academic Exploration of Sweet Myths

The Gingerbread Golem Grimoire: Sweet Magicks and Spells for the Festive Witch

The Curse of the Gingerbread Golem

10-minute Christmas Crafts for kids

<u>Christmas Crisis Solutions: The Ultimate Last-Minute Survival Guide</u>

Gingerbread Golem Recipes: Holiday Treats with a Magical Twist

The Infinite Key: Unlocking Mystical Secrets of the Ages

Enchanted Yule: A Wiccan and Pagan Guide to a Magical and Memorable Season

Dinosaurs of Power: Unlocking Ancient Magick

Astro-Dinos: The Cosmic Guide to Prehistoric Wisdom

Gallifrey's Yule Logs: A Festive Doctor Who Cookbook

The Dino Grimoire: Secrets of Prehistoric Magick

The Gift They Never Knew They Needed

The Gingerbread Golem's Culinary Alchemy: Enchanting Recipes for a Sweetly Dark Feast

A Time Lord Christmas: Holiday Adventures with the Doctor

Krampusproofing Your Home: Defensive Strategies for Yule

Silent Frights: A Collection of Christmas Creepypastas to Chill Your Bones

Santa Raptor's Jolly Carnage: A Dino-Claus Christmas Tale

Prehistoric Palettes: A Dino Wicca Coloring Journey

The Christmas Wishkeeper Chronicles

The Starlight Sleigh: A Holiday Journey

Elf Secrets: The True Magic of the North Pole

Candy Cane Conjurations

Cooking with Kids: Recipes Under 20 Minutes

Doctor Who: The TARDIS Confiscation

The Anxiety First Aid Kit: Quick Tools to Calm Your Mind

Frosty Whispers: A Winter's Tale

The Infinite Key: Unlocking the Secrets to Prosperity, Resilience, and Purpose

The Grasping Void: Why You'll Regret This Purchase
Astrology for Busy Bees: Star Signs Simplified
The Instant Focus Formula: Cut Through the Noise
The Secret Language of Colors: Unlocking the Emotional Codes
Sacred Fossil Chronicles: Blank Journal
The Christmas Cottage Miracle
Feeding Frenzy: Graboid-Inspired Recipes
Manifest in Minutes: The Quick Law of Attraction Guide
The Symbiote Chronicles: Doctor Who's Venomous Journey
Think Tiny, Grow Big: The Minimalist Mindset
The Energy Key: Unlocking Limitless Motivation
New Year, New Magic: Manifesting Your Best Year Yet
Unstoppable You: Mastering Confidence in Minutes
Infinite Energy: The Secret to Never Feeling Drained
Lightning Focus: Mastering the Art of Productivity in a Distracted World
Saturnalia Manifestation Magick: A Guide to Unlocking Abundance During the Solstice
Graboids and Garland: The Ultimate Tremors-Themed Christmas Guide
12 Nights of Holiday Magic
The Power of Pause: 60-Second Mindfulness Practices
The Quick Reset: How to Reclaim Your Life After Burnout
The Shadow Eater: A Tale of Despair and Survival
The Micro-Mastery Method: Transform Your Skills in Just Minutes a Day
Reclaiming Time: How to Live More by Doing Less
Chronovore: The Eternal Nexus
The Mind Reset: Unlocking Your Inner Peace in a Chaotic World
Confidence Code: Building Unshakable Self-Belief
Baby the Vampire Terrier
Baby the Vampire Terrier's Christmas Adventure
Celestial Streams: The Content Creator's Astrology Manual
The Wealth Whisperer: Unlocking Abundance with Everyday Actions
The Energy Equation: Maximize Your Output Without Burning Out
The Happiness Algorithm: Science-Backed Steps to Joyful Living
Stress-Free Success: Achieving Goals Without Anxiety
Mindful Wealth: The New Blueprint for Financial Freedom
The Festive Flavors of New Year: A Culinary Celebration
The Master's Gambit: Keys of Eternal Power
Shadowed Secrets: Groundhog Day Mysteries
Beneath the Burrow: Lessons from the Groundhog
Spring's Whispers: The Groundhog's Prediction
The Limitless Mindset: Unlock Your Untapped Potential
The Focus Funnel: How to Cut Through Chaos and Get Results

Bold Moves: Building Courage to Live on Your Terms
The Daily Shift: Simple Practices for Lasting Transformation
The Quarter-Life Reset: Thriving in Your 20s and 30s
The Art of Shadowplay: Building Your Own Personal Myth
The Eternal Loop: Finding Purpose in Repetition
Burrowing Wisdom: Life Lessons from the Groundhog
Shadow Work: A Groundhog Day Perspective
Love in Bloom: 5-Minute Romantic Gestures
The Shadowspell Codex: Secrets of Forbidden Magick
The Burnout Cure: Finding Balance in a Busy World
The Groundhog Prophecy: Unlocking Seasonal Secrets
Nog Tales: The Spirited History of Eggnog
Six More Weeks: Embracing Seasonal Transitions
The Lumivian Chronicles: Fragments of the Fifth Dimension
Money on Your Mind: A Beginner's Guide to Wealth
The Focus Fix: Breaking Through Distraction
January's Spirit Keepers: Mystical Protectors of the Cold
Creativity Unchained: Unlocking Your Wildest Ideas in 2025
Manifestation Mastery: 365 Days to Rewrite Your Reality
The Groundhog's Mirror: Reflecting on Change
The Weeping Angels' Christmas Curse
Burrowed in Time: A Groundhog Day Journey
Heartbeats: Poems to Share with Your Valentine
Dino Wicca: The Sacred Grimoire of Prehistoric Magick
Courage of the Pride: Finding Your Inner Roar
The Lion's Leap: Bold Moves for Big Results
Healthy Hustle: Achieving Without Overworking
Practical Manifesting: Turning Dreams into Reality in 2025
Jurassic Pharaohs: Unlocking the Magick of Ancient Egypt and Dino Wicca
The Happiness Equation: Small Changes for Big Joy
The Confidence Compass: Finding Your Inner Strength
Whispers in the Hollow: Tales of the Forgotten Beasts
Echoes from the Hollow: The Return of Forgotten Beasts
The Hollow Ascendant: The Rise of the Forgotten Beasts
The Relationship Reset: Building Better Connections
Mastering the Morning: How to Win the Day Before 8 AM
The Shadow's Dance: Groundhog Day Symbolism
Cupid's Kitchen: Quick Valentine's Day Recipes
Valentine's Day on a Budget: Love Without Breaking the Bank
Astrocraft: Aligning the Stars in the World of Minecraft
Forecasting Life: Groundhog Day Reflections

Bleeding Hearts: Twisted Tales of Valentine's Terror
Herbal Smoke Revolution: The Ultimate Guide to Nature's Cigarette Alternative
Winter's Wrath: The Complete Survival Blueprint for Extreme Freezes.
The Groundhog's Shadow: A Tale of Seasons
Burrowed Insights: Wisdom from the Groundhog
Sensual Strings: The Art of Erotic Bondage
Whispered Flames: Unlocking the Power of Fire Play
Forgotten Shadows: A Guide to Cryptids Lost to Time
Six Weeks of Secrets: Groundhog Day's Hidden Messages
Shadows and Cycles: Groundhog Day Reflections
The Art of Love Letters: Crafting the Perfect Message
Romantic Getaways at Home: Turning Your Space into Paradise
Purrfect Brews: A Cat Lover's Guide to Coffee and Companionship
The Groundhog's Wisdom: Timeless Lessons for Modern Life
The Shadow Oracle: Groundhog Day as a Predictor
Emerging from the Burrow: A Journey of Renewal
The Language of Love: Learning Your Partner's Love Style
Authorpreneur: The Ultimate Blueprint for Writing, Publishing, and Thriving as an Author
Weathering the Seasons: Groundhog Day Perspectives
Valentine's Day Magic: A Guide to Romantic Rituals
The Shadow Chronicles: Stories of Groundhog Day
Love and Laughter: Fun Games for Valentine's Day
AstroRealty: Unlocking the Stars for Property Success
The Groundhog's Path: A Guide to Seasonal Balance
Groundhog Day Diaries: Reflections in the Shadow
The Groundhog's Light: Illuminating the Path Ahead
Valentine's Traditions from Around the World
AI Wealth Revolution: Unlocking the Trillionaire Mindset
Love Rekindled: Reigniting Passion in Relationships
Single and Thriving: Self-Love on Valentine's Day
Emerald Legends: Mystical Tales of Ireland
Green Alchemy: Harnessing Nature's Magic
The Hearts of Horror: A Valentine's Day Nightmare
The Leprechaun's Guide to Wealth and Wisdom
Dancing with the Sidhe: Celebrating the Otherworld
Shamrocks and Shadows: Mysteries of the Green Isle
Emerald Energy: Harnessing Luck and Growth
The Gingerbread Golem's Valentine: A Sweetheart's Guide to Love and Enchantment
The Celtic Knot: Weaving Life and Destiny
Green Fire: Elemental Magic for St. Patrick's Day

Clover Chronicles: Finding Your Inner Luck
Ireland's Mystical Creatures: A Field Guide
Gingerbread Golem's Love Almanac
Prowl and Thrive: The Lion's Guide to Success
Love Alchemy: Transforming Your Life Through Heart Energy
WORLD DOMINATION: Woman's Rule 3:The New Life
The Midnight Rose: A Guide to Lunar Love Spells
The Forbidden Letters: Writing Your Own Love Prophecy
Luck and Lore: St. Patrick's Day for Modern Mystics
The Green Path: A Pagan Celebration of Renewal
The Dark Architect's Guide to Reprogramming Reality
Prankster's Paradise: A Guide to Harmless Hijinks
Manifest Your Reality: The Law of Attraction Simplified
The TARDIS Owner's Manual: Understanding the Doctor's Ship: *A complete guide to the TARDIS, its technology, secrets, and mysteries*
Starlit Romance: Astrology Secrets for Finding True Love
The Time Lord's Atlas: A Complete Guide to the Whoniverse: *A breakdown of the locations, planets, and dimensions explored in Doctor Who*
Sweetheart Shadows: The Dark Side of Love and Attraction
February Fire: Reigniting Passion in Every Area of Life
The Self-Love Toolkit: 5 Ways to Embrace Who You Are
February Sparks: Ignite Your Dreams in 28 Days
March to Success: A 31-Day Action Blueprint
Ancient Paths: The 13 Sacred Principles of Dino Wicca
Echoes of Tomorrow: Navigating the AI Revolution
The Wellness Blueprint: Balancing Mind, Body, and Soul
Green Horizons: Sustainable Living for a Better Tomorrow
The AI Wealth Code: How to Make Millions with Automation
AI-Powered Creativity: Writing, Art, and Music for Profit
Extinction Rites: Rebirthing Your Soul Through Prehistoric Magick
Sacred Serpents tarot
Celestial Enchantment blank journal
Star Strains
Culinary Journeys: Exploring Global Flavors at Home
The Hollowvale Curse
The Hollowvale Harvest
The Egg of Transformation: Awakening Your Inner Power
Blooming Into Power: A Wiccan Guide to Spring Awakening
The Nightmare Nexus: The Third Doctor's Perilous Haunting
Digital Detox: Reclaiming Your Life in a Connected World
Ostara's Path: Walking the Spiral of Renewal

The Sacred Hare
Financial Freedom: Building Wealth in the Modern Age
Spring's Cauldron: Stirring the Waters of Change
The Hollowvale Pact
Quantum Consciousness: The Science of Reality Shifting
The Hollowvale Hunger
The Sacred Waters Within: A Witch's Guide to Hydrocephalus Magick
The Raven's Nest: Building a Life of Unshakable Stability
AI and the Human Mind: The Future of Intelligence
The Hollowvale Reckoning
Timeless Love: Building and Maintaining Lasting Relationships
The Raven's Roar: Unlocking Unstoppable Confidence
Raven Sight: Awakening Intuition and Inner Wisdom
The Butterfly Effect: Small Changes, Big Transformations
Taming the Boogeyman: How to Conquer Your Inner Fears
The Magick of Green: Awakening Earth's Energy in You
The Entrepreneurial Mindset: Secrets to Business Success
The Hollowvale End
The Shadow Luck Ritual: Reclaiming Power from Your Dark Side
Spring Magick for Beginners: A Simple Guide to Seasonal Energy Work
Doctor Who: The Hollowvale Conundrum
The March of Miracles: Unlocking Synchronicities in Spring
Unveiling the Cosmos: A Guide to Stargazing and Space Exploration
The Ultimate Guide to Surviving an Economic Collapse
The AI Gold Rush: How to Profit from the AI Revolution
Bastet's Shadow: The Hidden Power of Feline Magick
The Bastet Codex: Unlocking the Goddess's Magickal Secrets
Purring Spells: Harnessing Bastet's Healing Frequencies
Bastet's Nine Lives: Rebirth, Transformation, and Immortality Spells
Primal Currents: Hydrocephalus Magick in the Path of Dino Wicca
The Digital Gold Rush: Mastering E-Commerce and Online Sales
Future Shock: Adapting to the Next Decade of Change
The Quantum Mindset: Think Like a Billionaire
Sacred Motherhood: Awakening the Divine Feminine Within
The Mother's Spellbook: Enchantments for Love, Protection, and Prosperity
The Witch's Guide to Parenting: Raising Empowered and Intuitive Children
The Magick of Motherhood: Reclaiming Your Power Through Rituals
The Pagan Path to Self-Love: A Goddess's Guide to Worth and Confidence
Wild Woman Magick: Unleashing Your Primal Power
The Money Magnet Blueprint: Unlocking Unlimited Wealth
Biohacking 101: Unlock Your Body's Full Potential

The Wild Father: A Pagan Guide to Strength and Wisdom

The Sacred Masculine: Unlocking Your Inner Power

The Druid's Compass

The Warrior's Mindset

The Father's Fire

Odin's Path

Ancestral Bonds

The House That Whispers

The Magician's Code

The Wild Hunt

The Green Man's Path

The Altar of Success

The Shadow and the Sword

The High Priestess's Guide to Energy Healing

The Lunar Mother

The Sacred Self-Care Grimoire

The Womb Wisdom Codex

The Wheel of the Mother

The Witch's Guide to Manifestation

The Q2 Reset

The Ultimate Guide to AI-Powered Passive Income

Escape the 9-5

AI Feline Fortunes

The Tear-Stained Grimoire

Razorblade Runes

Cemetery Sirens

The Midnight Wristwatch

The Town That Forgets

AI Horror & Creepypasta

The Hollow Frequency

The Breach Echo

The Quiet Between Worlds

The Sigil of Tharan-Khul

Summon the Vault of Y'ha'ten

The Becoming Codex

The Profit of Az'ra-nar

The Drowned Logos

Echoes of the Eldritch Will

The Deep Ledger

Necronomicon of Networth

Covenant of the Wealthwyrm

The Whisperer's Manifesto
The Rites of Azh-K'luth
The Ark of the Crawling Coin
The Tithe of Shadows
Inkheart Abyss
The Timewinds of Y'ha-nthlei
The Spiral Labyrinth of Azag-Nirrh
The Gallifreyan Heresy of the Black Pharaoh
The Psalms of Nyog-Sotha
Black Rain Alchemy
The Infinite Maw
The Entropic Blueprint
The Oracle of Sh'guul
The Book of Breach
The Drowned Saint's Testament
Dreamcraft of the Sleeper God
The Silence Market
Cthonomics: The Dark Wealth Algorithm
Invocation of the Ten-Eyed King
Wealthbound to the Wyrm Below
Become the Unnameable
Codex of the Sovereign Flame
Rituals of Relentless Becoming
The Shadow Ascends
The Eyes Beneath You
The Will That Wakes Worlds
Silence Is a Weapon
The Mirror That Screams
The Whisper Between Moments
The Mind That Devours Fear
The Myth of the Finished Self
The Architect of Your Madness
The Voice You've Buried
The Discipline of Madness
Stormborn: Awakening Your Inner Tempest
The Mind That Ate Time
Unbind Your Becoming
The Pact You Owe Yourself
The Devourer's Diet
The Acid That Carves the Path
The Tower You Must Burn

The Breath Between Worlds

Speak Like the Deep

The Labyrinth Within

The Spine of the Sea God

Rejection Is a Portal

The Crown You Refused

The Scar Is the Spell

The Lightless Flame

The Habit of Becoming Horrific

ChickenJockey Chaos

The Gatekeeper Within

You Are Not Your Name

The Compass of the Mad

The Archive of Unsent Letters

What the Mirror Can't Show You

The Knife You Needed

Worship Nothing, Become Everything

The Other Voice

The Body the World Forgot

The Vein of the Void

The Black Bone Codex

The Puzzle of the Hidden Self (Millennium Puzzle)

The Eye That Sees the Lie *(Millennium Eye)*

The Ring of Return (Millennium Ring)

The Rod of Relentless Will *(Millennium Rod)*

The Tally of the Soul (Millennium Tauk/Necklace)

The Key to the Locked Timeline (Millennium Key)

The Scale of Sacred Decisions (Millennium Scales)

Inferno Bites: The UnOfficial Minecraft Lava Cookbook

Rot in the Attic

Prana: The Hidden Force of Your Infinite Self

The Shadow Realm Within: Transforming Darkness Into Destiny

The Borderland Collapse

Claws of Protection: Bastet's Defensive Magick

Mr. Ring-a-Ding's Madness

Yugioh Astrology: Celestial Deckcraft and Duel Destiny (2026–2027 Edition)

The Seal You Signed: Unlocking the Power You Once Feared

The Puzzle of Infinite Minds: Unlocking the Mentalism Hidden Within

The Eye That Mirrors the All: Secrets of Inner Reflection

Doctor Who: The Toymaker's Broadcast

The Rod of Eternal Flow: Commanding the Currents of Vibration

Golden Eyes of Bastet: Enhancing Psychic Vision

The Key of Dual Forces: Balance Within the Polarity

The Scales of Living Rhythm: Timing the Dance of Life

The Necklace of Hidden Cause: Weaving the Webs of Fate

The Ring of Secret Masters: Rising Through the All Within All

Daggers of the Dying Deep

Bastet's Wealth and Fortune Magick: Prosperity Rituals of the Goddess

The Tide that Speaks

The Scrolls of Petosiris: 13 Rituals from the Feathered Eye

Petosiris and the Living Plague of Osirion

Feline Fire: Bastet's Passion and Love Magick

The Star Altar of Petosiris

Bastet's Whiskers: Supernatural Sensory Magick

The Bastet Grimoire

Feeding the Shadows

The Mouthless Prayer

The Spiral Wound

Becoming the Ibis: Lessons from Petosiris's Mind

The Crimson Coven: Cola Magick for Sweet Dominion

Sacred Cat's Paw

The Soda Zodiac: A Flavor for Every Sign

Covenant of the Crawling Flame

The Ink of Ish'Zur

Frothroot: The Thirst That Ate the World

The Golden Glyphs of Prosperity

The Etherbind Codex

Echoes of the Resistance: Reclaiming the You That Survived

Harnessed Minds: Breaking Free from Mental Control

The Eyes in the Smoke

Rootwake: The Carbon Covenant

Skitter Logic: Unlearning the Fear That Built You

Doctor Who: The World That Froths

Rootwake: The Fizz That Rewrites Flesh

Rootwake: Frothfather of the World

The Holly Pact: Blood Beneath the Mistletoe

The 2nd Mass Principle: Building Unbreakable Tribes

Web of Wits: A Survival Guide to Encounters with Anasi the Spider (Aunt Nancy)

The Hexbreaking Handbook: Effective Spells to Remove Curses

Pop Alchemy: Transform Your Life One Sip at a Time

The Mason Code: Leading in Unleadable Times

Petosiris and the Fifth Chamber of Thoth

The Ether Seed Within
The Parent of Tomorrow
Petosiris's Pyramid of Perpetual Wealth
Unlearn the World
Grimoire of the Hollow Tongue
Zodiac Weeds: Finding Your Strain Through the Stars

Get Some Tarot cards: https://www.makeplayingcards.com/sell/apophis-occult-shop

Get some shirts: https://www.bonfire.com/store/apophis-shirt-emporium/

<u>Instagrams:</u>
@apophis_enterprises,
@apophisbookemporium,
@apophisscardshop
Twitter: @apophisenterpr1
Tiktok:@apophisenterprise
Youtube: @sg1fan23477
Hive: @sg1fan23477
CheeLee: @SG1fan23477

Podcast: Apophis Chat Zone: https://open.spotify.com/show/5zXbr-CLEV2xzCp8ybrfHsk?si=fb4d4fdbdce44dec

Newsletter: https://apophiss-newsletter-27c897.beehiiv.com/

If you want to support me or see posts of other projects that I have come over to: **buymeacof-fee.com/mpetchinskg**

I post there daily several times a day

Get your Dinowicca or Christmas themed digital products, especially Santa Raptor songs and other musics. Here: **https://sg1fan23477.gumroad.com**

Apophis Yuletide Digital has not only digital Christmas items, but it will have all things with Dinowicca as well as other Digital products.